My
Kindle Fire HD

Jim Cheshire
Jennifer Kettell

que®

800 East 96th Street,
Indianapolis, Indiana 46240 USA

My Kindle Fire HD

Copyright © 2013 by Pearson Education, Inc.

ISBN-13: 978-0-7897-5322-9
ISBN-10: 0-7897-5322-7

Library of Congress Cataloging-in-Publication data is on file.

Printed in the United States of America

Second Printing: November 2013

Trademarks

Warning and Disclaimer

Bulk Sales

Que Publishing offers excellent discounts on this book when ordered in quantity for bulk purchases or special sales. For more information, please contact

U.S. Corporate and Government Sales
1-800-382-3419
corpsales@pearsontechgroup.com

For sales outside of the U.S., please contact

International Sales
international@pearsoned.com

Editor-in-Chief
Greg Wiegand

Executive Editor
Loretta Yates

Development Editor
Todd Brakke

Managing Editor
Sandra Schroeder

Senior Project Editor
Tonya Simpson

Copy Editor
Krista Hansing

Indexer
Erika Millen

Proofreader
Gill Editorial Services

Technical Editor
Greg Kettell

Publishing Coordinator
Cindy Teeters

Book Designer
Compositor
Tricia Bronkella

Contents at a Glance

	Introduction	1
Chapter 1	Getting Started with the Kindle Fire	9
Chapter 2	Loading Your Kindle Fire	43
Chapter 3	Using Amazon's Manage Your Kindle Page	79
Chapter 4	Reading on the Kindle Fire	99
Chapter 5	Managing Content with Calibre	137
Chapter 6	Accessing and Listening to Music	155
Chapter 7	Watching Video on Your Kindle Fire	177
Chapter 8	Installing and Using Apps	201
Chapter 9	Using Social Media and Chat	225
Chapter 10	Reading and Sending E-mail	249
Chapter 11	Managing Your Personal Documents and Data	271
Chapter 12	Browsing the Web with Silk	283
Chapter 13	Giving Your Kids a Kindle Fire	303
	Index	319

Table of Contents

Introduction   1

An Overview of the Various Kindle Fire Models   2
What's New on the Kindle Fire   4
What You'll Find in This Book   4
How to Navigate This Book   5
Let's Light This Fire   7

1 Getting Started with the Kindle Fire   9

The Hardware   10
Initial Setup   12
    Connecting to a Listed Wi-Fi Network   12
    Connecting to an Unlisted Wi-Fi Network   13
    Setting Your Time Zone   14
    Registering with Amazon   15
    Connecting to Facebook and Twitter   16
Basic Usage of the Kindle Fire   17
The Home Screen   19
    Downloading Items   20
    Removing Downloaded Items from Your Kindle Fire   22
    Adding an Item to Favorites   23
    Removing an Item from Favorites   24
    Rearranging Favorites   24
    Changing the Screen Timeout   25
Notifications and Options   26
    Notifications   27
    Options   27
Settings   28
    Locking the Screen Orientation   28
    Adjusting the Volume   29
    Adjusting Screen Brightness   30
    Checking Device Information   30
    Turning Off Wi-Fi   32

Using the Keyboard..32

Entering Text..33

Positioning the Cursor..33

Selecting and Editing Text......................................34

Copying/Cutting and Pasting Text........................35

Entering Punctuation and Numbers......................35

Adding Accent Marks and Diacriticals..................36

Connecting to Other Hardware....................................37

Adding Bluetooth Accessories................................37

Searches...38

Searching Your Library..39

Searching the Web..39

Searching Amazon Stores..40

2 Loading Your Kindle Fire   43

Amazon Prime..44

Setting Up Amazon Prime..45

Amazon Cloud Drive..47

Accessing Your Cloud Drive.....................................49

Creating Folders..50

Deleting Folders..51

Recovering Deleted Items..52

Adding Files to Your Cloud Drive............................52

Downloading the Cloud Drive Application..............53

Accessing Cloud Drive Files from Your Kindle Fire...54

Saving Files to Your Device.....................................55

Amazon Cloud Player..57

Launching Cloud Player...58

Importing Your Music..58

Playing Music on Your Computer.............................61

Creating Playlists..62

Downloading Songs to Your Kindle Fire..................63

Changing How Amazon Handles Purchased Music....65

Amazon Instant Video 66

    Getting Videos from Amazon Instant Video 67

Kindle Reader Applications and Kindle Cloud Reader 68

    Accessing Kindle Reader Applications 69

    Accessing Kindle Cloud Reader 70

    Opening and Downloading Books 71

    Reading Books on the Kindle Cloud Reader 73

Transferring Files from Your Computer 74

    Transferring Files from a PC 75

    Transferring Files from a Mac 76

3 Using Amazon's Manage Your Kindle Page   79

Managing Your Books and Docs 80

    Accessing Manage Your Kindle 80

    Viewing Books and Docs 81

    Sending Books and Docs to Your Kindle 82

    Downloading Books to a Computer 83

    Deleting Books and Docs 84

    Changing Your Kindle E-mail Address 85

    Adding an Approved E-mail for Docs 86

    Disabling Doc Archiving 87

Managing Subscriptions 87

    Changing Where a Subscription Is Delivered 88

    Canceling a Subscription 88

    Reactivating a Canceled Subscription 89

    Changing Subscription Privacy Settings 91

Updating Kindle Payment Information 91

    Changing Amazon Purchases Credit Cards 91

    Changing Current Subscriptions Credit Cards 93

Managing Your Kindle Devices 94

    Deregistering a Kindle 94

    Renaming Your Kindle Fire 95

    Deregistering a Kindle App 96

    Turning Off Whispersync 96

    Turning Off Special Offers 97

4 Reading on the Kindle Fire   99

Finding Content 99
Buying Books 100
Purchasing After Sampling 101
Using the Kindle Lending Library 102
Lending Books to Friends and Family 103
Subscribing to Periodicals 104
Organizing Your Books 105
Browsing Your Library 106
Downloading a Book to Your Device 106
Removing a Book from Your Device 107
Reading on Your Kindle 108
Reading a Book 108
Navigating a Book 109
Changing Font Styles 111
Looking Up Definitions 112
Working with Notes and Highlights 113
Adding a Note 114
Viewing an Individual Note 115
Editing a Note 115
Deleting a Note 116
Adding a Highlight 116
Viewing All Notes and Highlights 117
Deleting a Highlight 118
Working with Bookmarks 119
Adding a Bookmark 119
Removing a Bookmark 119
Moving to a Bookmark 120
Reading Magazines and Newspapers 121
Reading a Page View–Enabled Magazine 121
Reading in Text View and Reading Newspapers ... 123
Listening to Audiobooks 125
Downloading Audiobooks 125
Listening to Audiobooks 126
Setting a Sleep Timer 128

Immersion Reading 128

Using Text-to-Speech 130

Searching Content and Accessing Reference Materials 131

Using X-Ray for Books 131

Searching the Current Item 132

Searching Wikipedia or Google from Books 134

5 Managing Content with Calibre   137

Getting Started with Calibre 138

Using the Welcome Wizard 139

Adding Content to Calibre 140

Importing Books 140

Searching for New eBooks 141

Editing Book Information 143

Downloading Metadata 143

Manually Editing Metadata 146

Transferring eBooks to the Kindle Fire 147

Converting to MOBI Format 148

Deleting Non-MOBI Formats 149

Transferring an eBook to Your Kindle 150

E-mailing eBooks to Your Kindle 151

6 Accessing and Listening to Music   155

Browsing and Downloading Your Music 155

Browsing Artists 156

Scrolling Quickly in Music 158

Monitoring Downloads from an Album 158

Monitoring All Music Downloads 159

Canceling Downloads 160

Searching for Music 160

Searching Your Music Collection 161

Playing Music 161

Listening to Music 162

Accessing Music Controls 163

Managing Playlists 164
  Creating a Playlist 164
  Editing a Playlist 165
  Adding Artists or Albums to a Playlist 166
  Playing a Playlist 167
  Downloading a Playlist 167
  Renaming a Playlist 169
  Deleting a Playlist 169
Buying New Music 170
  Navigating the Music Store 170
  Sampling and Buying Music 171
  Changing Music Delivery Preferences 173

7   Watching Video on Your Kindle Fire   177

Navigating the Video Store 177
  Browsing the Video Store 178
  Viewing Movie Details 179
  Renting or Purchasing a Movie 181
  Viewing TV Show Details 182
  Buying TV Shows by Episode 184
  Purchasing Complete TV Show Seasons 185
  Purchasing a TV Show from Prime Instant Video 185
  Buying a Season TV Pass 187
Working with Your Video Library 189
  Watching a Movie or TV Show 189
  Using X-Ray for Video 191
  Adding a Video to Your Watchlist 192
  Downloading Movies 194
  Downloading a TV Show 195
  Removing a Downloaded Video 196
Sideloading Videos 196
  Copying Video to Your Kindle Fire 197
  Watching Sideloaded Videos 198
  Deleting Sideloaded Videos 199

8 Installing and Using Apps **201**

The Appstore 201

Browsing Apps 202

Viewing and Purchasing Apps 203

Viewing Saved or Recently Viewed Apps 205

Viewing Subscriptions 206

Your Apps Library 207

Browsing Your Apps Library 207

Installing a Purchased App 208

Adding an App to Favorites 209

Uninstalling an App 210

Updating an Application 210

Application Settings 212

Force-Stopping an Application 212

Clearing Application Data 214

Indispensable Apps 215

Evernote 216

Pandora 217

ES File Explorer 219

Games for Your Kindle Fire 220

Accessing Games 221

9 Using Social Media and Chat **225**

Sharing with Facebook, Twitter, and the Kindle
Community 225

Setting Up Your Social Networks 226

Sharing General Comments About Books 228

Sharing Highlights from Books 229

Before You Go in Books 230

Importing Your Facebook Photos 231

Using the Facebook App 232

Video Chatting over Skype 234

Setting Up Skype 235

Adding Skype Contacts 237

Making a Call with Skype 238

Sharing Game Achievements with GameCircle 239

Identifying GameCircle Games 240

Creating a GameCircle Profile 241

Adding Friends on GameCircle 242

Accessing Game Achievements 243

Accessing Leaderboards 244

Viewing Game Summaries 246

10 Reading and Sending E-mail   249

E-mail Accounts 249

Accessing the Add Account Page 250

Adding a Gmail, Hotmail, AOL, or Yahoo! Account ... 251

Adding a POP3 or IMAP Account 253

Modifying Your Account Settings 257

Removing an Account 260

Managing Your E-mail Inbox 261

Choosing an Inbox 261

Choosing a Folder 262

Searching E-mail 263

Synchronizing E-mail and Loading More Messages ... 264

Selecting and Managing Multiple Messages 265

Reading E-mail 266

Reading a Message 266

Viewing Attachments 267

Composing a New E-mail Message 268

11 Managing Your Personal Documents and Data   271

Managing Personal Documents 271

Viewing PDF Documents 272

Viewing Word Documents 274

Viewing Spreadsheets 275

Using the Contacts App 277

Viewing Contacts 277

Adding a Contact 278

Editing a Contact 280

Changing Contact Sort Order and Name Display 280

12 Browsing the Web with Silk   283

Browsing the Web 283

Using the Starter Page 284

Browsing to a Website 285

Navigating a Page 285

Sharing Pages on Facebook 287

Sharing Pages with E-mail 288

Copying a Link to the Current Page 288

Copying a Hyperlink on a Page 289

Searching in the Current Page 290

Searching the Web 291

Working with Tabs 291

Opening Links in a New Tab 292

Navigating Tabs 292

Using Bookmarks and History 293

Bookmarking the Current Page 293

Bookmarking a Hyperlink 294

Viewing and Following Bookmarks 295

Editing a Bookmark 295

Viewing History 296

Downloading Files 297

Starting and Monitoring Downloads 297

Sharing Downloaded Files 298

Deleting Downloaded Files 299

Configuring Silk Settings 300

Setting Your Search Engine 300

Enable Location 301

13 Giving Your Kids a Kindle Fire   303

Setting Up Kindle FreeTime 303

Accessing Kindle FreeTime 304

Setting Up Child Profiles 305

Manage Content on FreeTime 306

Setting Daily Time Limits 308

Changing the Parental Controls Password 309

Teaching Your Kids How to Use Kindle FreeTime 311

Using the FreeTime Interface 312

Navigation for Nonreaders 313

Exiting FreeTime 314

Parental Controls for Older Children 314

Setting a Parental Controls Password 315

Managing Parental Controls Settings 316

Index   **319**

About the Author

Jim Cheshire has been writing about the Kindle since the very first Kindle device was released. Jim is an expert on technical devices such Amazon's Kindle, Windows Phone, and Windows 8, as well as Web design and programming. Jim has written a dozen books on these topics and also shares his passion and knowledge with readers via online columns and articles. Jim helps developers make the most of Microsoft technologies. When he's not working, Jim spends time enjoying his family and especially loves spending time outdoors.

Jennifer Kettell has written and contributed to dozens of books about software applications, web design, and digital photography. She also writes fiction. When Jenn isn't writing, she can usually be found with her Kindle, reading almost a book a day. Jenn has lived all over the United States but currently calls upstate New York home. Visit her website at www.jenniferkettell.com.

Dedication

To my extended "family" at Adirondack TKD for their love and support. My life is so much richer for having all of you in it.

Acknowledgments

My deepest gratitude and thanks to the many people at Que Publishing who have worked so hard to support me. I'm grateful to Loretta Yates for inviting me to write this book and making roadblocks seem like minor potholes. Huge thanks to Todd Brakke for his editing and sense of humor. Thanks also to Tonya Simpson and Krista Hansing for their production and copyediting expertise. Finally, I just can't put into words how much I appreciate Greg Kettell for reviewing the technical content of this book moments after I finished each chapter—and for pitching in with everything else around the house so I had more writing time.

We Want to Hear from You!

As the reader of this book, *you* are our most important critic and commentator. We value your opinion and want to know what we're doing right, what we could do better, what areas you'd like to see us publish in, and any other words of wisdom you're willing to pass our way.

We welcome your comments. You can email or write to let us know what you did or didn't like about this book—as well as what we can do to make our books better.

Please note that we cannot help you with technical problems related to the topic of this book.

When you write, please be sure to include this book's title and author as well as your name and e-mail address. We will carefully review your comments and share them with the author and editors who worked on the book.

Email: feedback@quepublishing.com

Mail: Que Publishing
        ATTN: Reader Feedback
        800 East 96th Street
        Indianapolis, IN 46240 USA

Reader Services

Visit our website and register this book at quepublishing.com/register for convenient access to any updates, downloads, or errata that might be available for this book.

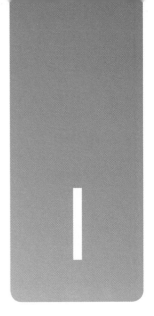

Introduction

You might have purchased your Kindle Fire primarily to read books, but the device you hold in your hands can do so much more. After you connect to the Internet and register the Kindle Fire with your Amazon.com account, you'll quickly fill it with books, music, videos, apps, and games. You'll use it to browse the Web. You'll even add your own photos and personal documents, making your Kindle Fire uniquely yours.

That's not to say that the Kindle Fire isn't good for reading. You'll have access to millions of books on Amazon.com and other websites, many of them free or less than $1.99. You can borrow books from your local library. When reading is inconvenient, such as when you're driving, you can even have your Kindle Fire read to you, either with an audiobook or using text-to-speech. You're also not limited to books; you can read magazines and newspapers as well.

The Kindle Fire is primarily intended for consuming content—that is, for reading, listening, or watching. Much of that content is stored in the *cloud*, on Amazon's servers, and you access it over a Wi-Fi or 4G connection. Even if you download content to your device, at which point it becomes device content, a copy stays in the cloud so that it remains accessible from other devices—or if you need to download a new copy. If that all that sounds a bit confusing right now, don't worry! Everything will become clear after you read this book.

An Overview of the Various Kindle Fire Models

Other Kindle devices are dedicated e-readers, but the Kindle Fire is also a multimedia entertainment device and a tablet computer. Four models of the Kindle Fire exist. All four have the same user interface and access to more than 22 million books, movies, songs, magazines, audiobooks, TV shows, games, and apps. Each model also offers free, unlimited cloud storage for your Amazon content. The processor, display, and storage vary for each model, however, as noted here:

Camera

View all your Amazon content from the Carousel.

Access Quick Links or similar content.

Click for Favorites.

- **Kindle Fire:** This is the second generation of the base Kindle Fire model. The new model is 40 percent faster than its predecessor, with twice the memory and longer battery life. It has a 7-inch LCD display with a resolution of 1024×600 pixels. (That's not quite HD.) The device offers 8GB of memory with a 1.2GHz dual-core processor. Unlike the other three models of the Kindle Fire, this device does not have a forward-facing camera. This base model also offers Wi-Fi connectivity but lacks the dual-band, dual-antenna of the higher-end models. The Kindle Fire's battery can handle up to 8.5 hours of continuous use. The Kindle Fire costs $159.

- **Kindle Fire HD:** Although it has the same 7-inch screen size as the base model, the Kindle Fire HD packs more power into its small space. It comes with an HD LCD display with 1280×800 resolution and up to 720p HD. It offers the same 1.2GHz dual-core processor, but it comes with either 16GB or 32GB of storage. The stereo speakers are better on the HD models, with Dolby Digital Plus audio, which automatically optimizes the audio based on whether you're listening to music or watching a movie. The Kindle Fire HD connects with dual-band, dual-antenna Wi-Fi for a faster and more reliable connection. The battery lasts for up to 11 hours of continuous use. The Kindle Fire HD costs $199 for the 16GB version and $249 for the 32GB model.

- **Kindle Fire HD 8.9-inch:** Want a larger display? As its name implies, this model comes with an 8.9-inch HD LCD display with 1920×1200 resolution and up to 1,080p HD. The other major difference is that the HD 8.9-inch model has a 1.5GHz processor. The Kindle Fire HD 8.9-inch costs $299 for the 16GB version and $369 for the 32GB version.

- **Kindle Fire HD 8.9-inch 4G:** As its name implies, this top-of-the-line model offers 4G LTE connectivity in addition to Wi-Fi. Amazon offers annual data plans through AT&T for $49.99 per year for 250MB of data per month (plans offering 3GB or 5GB data usage are also available). The Kindle Fire HD 8.9-inch 4G has the same 1.5GHz processor as the other 8.9-inch model, but it comes with either 32GB or 64GB of storage on the device and offers additional cloud storage for your personal documents and photos. The 32GB version of the Kindle Fire HD 8.9-inch 4G costs $499, and the 64GB model costs $599.

What's New on the Kindle Fire

No matter which Kindle Fire model you choose, you will find plenty to do with it. If you're upgrading from the first-generation Kindle Fire, you will be happy to discover many new features. In addition to the upgrades in display, processor, and other hardware enhancements, the new Kindle Fire offers many other improvements.

- Upgraded operating system. If you're of a technical bent, the Kindle Fire uses a proprietary version of Android 4.0 (Ice Cream Sandwich). For the rest of us, it's enough to know that the operating system is faster and smoother.

- Improved battery life in the base Kindle Fire model.

- Physical volume-control buttons on the device, to save you from having to navigate to the volume controls on the screen.

- A front-facing camera that enables video chat over Skype and other apps (not available on the base Kindle Fire).

- Integration with Facebook and Twitter.

- Kindle FreeTime, which provides parental control over what kids can do on the Kindle Fire and the hours during which they can do it.

- A micro-HDMI port to connect the Kindle Fire with an external display (not available on the base Kindle Fire).

All Kindle Fire models also come with a free month of Amazon Prime, if you don't already have an account. Amazon Prime offers unlimited streaming of more than 25,000 movies and TV shows, making it easy to watch a show wherever you have Wi-Fi (or 4G) access. Prime also lets you borrow one free title a month from the Kindle Owners' Lending Library. And if you shop on Amazon.com, you can get free two-day shipping on most items as part of your Prime membership.

What You'll Find in This Book

The Kindle Fire is a tablet computer for people who aren't necessarily computer geeks and who just want to be entertained, read a good book, or have fun—and might have the occasional need to get some work done. *My Kindle Fire* was written with that same mindset. I show you how to get the most fun out of your Kindle Fire, and teach you how to access your personal documents when you need to work. Of course, if you are a computer geek, this book can help you as well.

This book covers all the capabilities of your Kindle Fire. I cover each feature using a step-by-step approach, complete with figures that correspond to each step. You never have to wonder what or where to tap. Each task shows you how to interact with your Kindle Fire using simple symbols that illustrate what you should do.

This icon means that you tap and hold an object on the screen.

This icon means that you drag an item on the screen.

This icon indicates that you pinch on the screen.

This icon means that you spread your thumb and finger on the screen.

This icon indicates that you swipe on the screen.

Along the way, I add plenty of tips that help you better understand a feature or task. If you want to dig deeper, you'll appreciate the Go Further sidebars that provide a more in-depth look at certain features. I also warn you of problems and pitfalls with particular tasks with It's Not All Good sidebars.

How to Navigate This Book

There is a lot to discover about your Kindle Fire. The major functions might be visible to the naked eye, but a lot more hides beneath the surface. As you read this book, you might be surprised to find that your Kindle Fire does more than you ever imagined.

Here are the topics we'll cover in this book.

- Chapter 1, "Getting Started with the Kindle Fire," explains how to set up your device and access the most common settings. You also learn how to operate your Kindle Fire and use the onscreen keyboard. Finally, you learn how to set up external devices such as a Bluetooth keyboard and share your screen with an external display.

- Chapter 2, "Loading Your Kindle Fire," covers Amazon's cloud services and other ways to transfer content onto your Kindle Fire.

- Chapter 3, "Using Amazon's Manage Your Kindle Page," shows you how to access the Manage Your Kindle page on the Internet, where you can review your Kindle library, rename your Kindle Fire, manage all your Kindle devices and Kindle apps, and much more.

- Chapter 4, "Reading on the Kindle Fire," describes how to find reading material and take advantage of the Kindle Fire's powerful features for reading books, newspapers, magazines, and more.

- Chapter 5, "Managing Content with Calibre," introduces you to Calibre, a free application that helps you manage your eBook library, including books you get from sources other than directly through Amazon. It even helps you convert them to the proper format and transfer them onto your Kindle Fire.

- Chapter 6, "Accessing and Listening to Music," shows you how to use your Kindle Fire to play music in your music library (both on your device and in the cloud) and use Amazon's MP3 Store to add to your music collection. You also learn about using playlists and other, more advanced features.

- Chapter 7, "Watching Video on Your Kindle," covers using your Kindle Fire to stream and download videos from Amazon's video store. You also learn how to convert your own videos to play them on your Kindle Fire.

- Chapter 8, "Installing and Using Apps," introduces you to the world of apps that dramatically increase the functionality of your Kindle Fire. You learn how to find and install apps, as well as how to deal with misbehaving apps. You also discover some apps that you should definitely install on your Kindle Fire.

- Chapter 9, "Using Social Media and Chat," shows you how to access Facebook and Twitter to stay connected with your friends and how to video chat with them using the Skype app. You also learn how to connect to Game Circle to challenge your friends and compare scores.

- Chapter 10, "Reading and Sending E-mail," shows you how to use your Kindle Fire to read and send e-mail. You also learn how to handle attachments in e-mail.

- Chapter 11, "Managing Your Personal Documents and Data," covers loading, viewing, and editing your personal documents and photos on the Kindle Fire. You also learn how to add and manage contacts.

- Chapter 12, "Browsing the Web with Silk," walks you through using Silk, the web browser that comes with your Kindle Fire. You learn how to access websites, use bookmarks and tabs, and control Silk's behavior.

- Chapter 13, "Giving Your Kids a Kindle Fire," describes how to set up Kindle FreeTime to establish time limits and restrict the content your children can access from their Kindle Fire. I also recommend some good apps for kids.

Let's Light This Fire

If you've already gone through the initial setup of your Kindle Fire, you might be tempted to skip ahead to Chapter 2 at this point. I urge you to avoid the the rush and at least skim Chapter 1. You won't want to miss the hidden gems in Chapter 1.

Now that the stage is set, let's light up your Kindle Fire!

View content in
each category

Swipe down to
access Settings

Jennifer's 5th Kindle 11:57

Search

Shop Games Apps Books Music Videos Ne

IMD

View your
Amazon
content
from the
Carousel

Quick Links

New Message This Week Favorite Contacts

Access
Quick
Links for
Apps

Tap to see
Favorites

In this chapter, you learn how to connect your Kindle Fire to your Wi-Fi network and register it with Amazon, and you discover the basics of navigating and using your tablet. Topics include the following:

→ The hardware

→ Initial setup

→ Basic usage of the Kindle Fire

→ The home screen

→ Notifications and options

→ Settings

→ Using the keyboard

→ Connecting to other hardware

→ Searches

Getting Started with the Kindle Fire

The Kindle Fire is unassuming at first glance. However, after you power it up, you soon realize that it opens up a new world of entertainment and information. Couple it with Amazon's wide range of services, and the Kindle Fire becomes a truly extraordinary device. In fact, in addition to being a great reading device, your Kindle Fire might replace your computer for some of the things you do on the Internet, especially when you're away from home.

The Kindle Fire is not difficult to use. Many of its features are intuitive, and you can easily discover many of the great tasks it can do just by playing with it. However, if this is your first tablet, you should be familiar with some essentials to get the most from the device. This chapter starts you on the right foot by teaching you about the basic operation of the Kindle Fire.

The Hardware

Your Kindle Fire is equipped with a power button on the top of the device when in portrait mode (holding the Kindle Fire with the camera on the left side). Press and release this button to power on your Kindle Fire. If the Kindle Fire is already turned on, a quick press of the power button puts it to sleep. Many Kindle Fire covers automatically turn on the device when opened and put it to sleep when closed. Pressing and holding the power button enables you to power off your Kindle Fire.

Should You Power Off?

The display on your Kindle Fire is the primary power consumer on the device. Therefore, your Kindle Fire uses much less power when it's in sleep mode. Obviously, turning it off completely uses even less power, but if you subscribe to a magazine or a newspaper, you won't get your subscription automatically when your Kindle Fire is turned off.

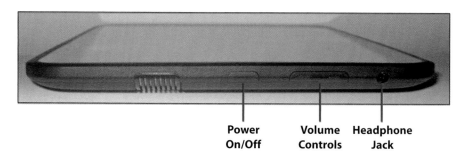

**Power
On/Off**   **Volume
Controls**   **Headphone
Jack**

To the left of the power button is the volume up/down button. Press the left side of the button to raise the volume, and press the right side to lower it. If you want to use headphones or external speakers while listening to music or video, plug them into the 1/4-inch audio plug to the right of the volume controls.

On the right side of the device (if you're holding it in portrait mode, with the camera on the left) is a micro-USB port for charging your Kindle Fire. The Kindle Fire comes with a cable to connect it to a computer so that you can charge the device from your computer's power. You can also separately purchase a wall charger, which charges the Kindle Fire faster and can be used when you're away from your computer.

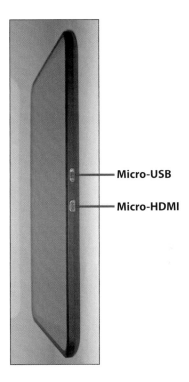

Below the micro-USB port is a micro-HDMI port. The micro-HDMI port is used to connect the Kindle Fire to a television or other display and is useful when you want to watch a movie or TV show on a larger screen. You learn how to make this connection later in this chapter.

At the top and bottom of your Kindle Fire are dual stereo speakers. If you hold your Kindle Fire in landscape position, the speakers are on either side of the device, making watching movies and TV shows a much more enjoyable audio experience.

It's Not All Good

Charging the Kindle Fire

The Kindle Fire ships with a micro-USB-to-USB cable. You can use this cable to connect your Kindle Fire to your computer so that you can transfer files and charge the device. Fully charging your Kindle Fire using this cable takes 11 hours. If you want to cut this to less than 5 hours, you must spend an extra $19.99 to purchase an Amazon Kindle PowerFast adapter. This charger plugs directly into a wall outlet instead of using your computer as a charging conduit.

Initial Setup

When you first turn on your Kindle Fire, you see the lock screen. This screen is usually an ad for a book or other form of Amazon content. Swipe your finger across the lock from right to left to unlock the device. You then go through a series of steps that get you started using your new device.

Kindle Fire Updates

It's possible that your Kindle Fire won't have the latest version of the Kindle operating system. If it doesn't, the latest version is downloaded and installed automatically when you set up your Kindle Fire for the first time.

Connecting to a Listed Wi-Fi Network

To access content on your Kindle Fire, you need to connect to a Wi-Fi network, which is where the initial setup process begins.

1. Tap the name of your Wi-Fi network.

2. Enter the password for your Wi-Fi network.

3. Tap Connect.

Manually Connecting to a Wi-Fi Network

If you need to return to the Wi-Fi setup or want to set up an additional Wi-Fi connection, first tap the time and pull down to open the Quick Settings and then tap Wi-Fi.

>>Go Further

COMPLETE SETUP LATER

If you're anxious to play with your Kindle Fire without having to go through all the setup motions, use the Complete Setup Later option that appears at the bottom of the Connect to a Wi-Fi Network screen. Because this aborts the entire setup process, you must manually go into the My Account option in Settings to register your Kindle Fire with your Amazon account to gain access to the Amazon Cloud. You also must set up a connection in the Wireless option in Settings before you can connect to the Internet. My advice is to be patient and go through the entire setup procedure right away.

Connecting to an Unlisted Wi-Fi Network

If your network's name isn't listed, you might need to manually enter the information necessary to connect to your Wi-Fi network.

1. Tap Enter Other Wi-Fi Network at the bottom of the network list.

2. Enter the name (SSID) of your network.

3. Tap the type of security that your network uses.

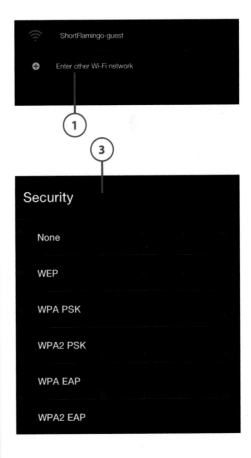

4. Enter the password for your network, if necessary.

5. Tap Save.

If you are fortunate enough to own a Kindle Fire HD 8.9-inch 4G, you can find instructions for setting up your 4G service at the website that accompanies this book. The URL for this site is www.informit.com/title/9780789750716.

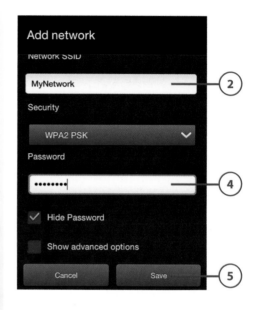

Setting Your Time Zone

Your Kindle Fire doesn't have a GPS, so it can't determine your time zone automatically. You need to select your time zone during setup.

1. Tap your time zone.

2. If your time zone isn't listed, tap Select Another Time Zone to see a list of additional time zones.

3. Tap Continue.

Registering with Amazon

Your Kindle Fire must be registered with an Amazon account so that you can access content. If your Kindle is not already registered to your Amazon account, you need to do that next.

Is Your Kindle Already Registered?

If you ordered your Kindle Fire from your own Amazon account, it will be preregistered before Amazon ships the device to you. If you received your Kindle Fire as a gift or purchased it at a retail store, you will need to register the device before you can access content.

1. Enter your e-mail address that is registered with Amazon.

2. Enter your Amazon password.

3. Tap Register.

Don't Have an Amazon Account?

If you don't already have an Amazon account, you can create one online at Amazon.com or you can tap Create Account at the bottom of the Register Your Kindle screen to create one.

4. Your Kindle confirms that it is now registered to your account. Tap Continue.

Connecting to Facebook and Twitter

Your Kindle Fire can help you stay connected to your social networks. If you enter your username and passwords during the initial setup, the Facebook and Twitter apps are automatically configured for you.

1. Select Connect Your Facebook Account.

2. Enter your e-mail address.

3. Enter your password.

4. Tap connect.

5. Repeat steps 1–4 for Twitter. Tap Get Started Now when you're done.

You've reached the end of the guided setup. Congratulations! After you complete the initial setup, the Kindle Fire guides you through a series of screens that describe some of the basic usability features of the tablet. And now you're ready to play.

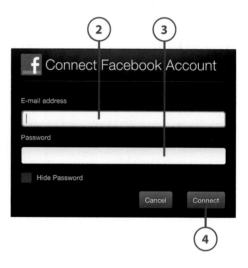

Basic Usage of the Kindle Fire

By now, you're already familiar with tapping to select buttons and other items on your Kindle Fire. You can also use several other gestures to interact with your Kindle Fire.

Canceling a Tap

Taps are registered when you lift your finger from the screen. If you tap something by mistake and you want to cancel the tap, slide your finger onto another part of the screen before lifting it.

In addition to tapping to select items, you can double-tap to do things such as zoom in on a figure in a book or a website. To do this, tap your finger on the same point on the screen twice in quick succession.

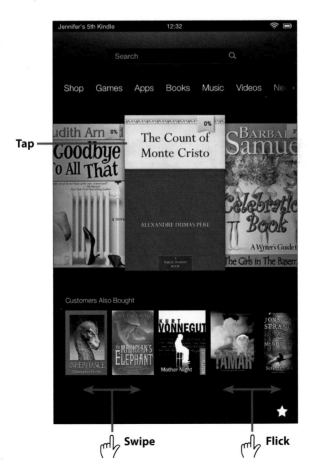

You can scroll through lists of items both horizontally and vertically by swiping your finger. Hold your finger on the list and move it up and down or left and right to scroll through items. To quickly scroll, flick your finger in the direction you want to scroll as you remove your finger from the screen.

To incrementally zoom in and out, you can use pinch and reverse pinch gestures. This is typically used on pictures, websites, and subscription content, but many applications also allow you to use this gesture.

To zoom in, place your thumb and index finger on the screen close together and move them apart (reverse pinching). To zoom out, place your thumb and index finger on the screen with some distance between them and move them together (pinching).

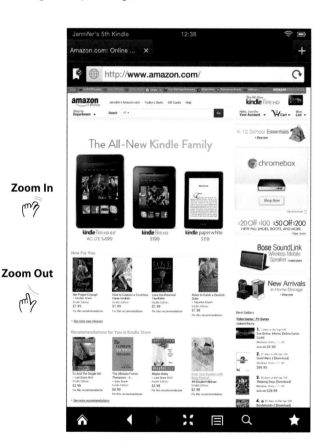

The Home Screen

After you complete the initial setup, press the Home button (the one that looks like a house) to get to the home screen. The Carousel contains thumbnails for your books and recently accessed content and websites. Swipe or flick across the Carousel to browse the items available there. Tapping an item opens that item. You can't change the order of items in the Carousel; the most recently accessed items always appear first.

The Navigation menu provides quick access to the various content libraries available on the Kindle Fire. If you select a specific content library, the Carousel shows content from only that library. Swipe or flick across the Navigation menu to see additional categories of content.

The Quick Links bar provides thumbnails of content related to the content in the center of the Carousel. If the Carousel displays a book at the center, for example, the Quick Links show books that other readers of that book have purchased through Amazon. Some apps provide Quick Links to tasks within that app. If the Carousel is focused on the E-mail app, as shown here, the Quick Links provide options to send a new message or view your Favorite Contacts.

Application-Related Quick Links

Downloading Items

The Carousel displays both items on your Kindle Fire (called *device items*) and items that you've previously purchased that are in your online library (called *cloud items*). If you want to open a cloud item, you first need to download it to your device.

1. Swipe to the item you want to download.

2. Tap the item to download it to your device.

3. While the item is downloading, you can tap the X to cancel the download. After an item has been downloaded, it is a device item and can be accessed at any time, even when the Kindle Fire is not connected to Wi-Fi.

FINDING YOUR ITEMS

The Carousel on the home screen shows a mix of cloud and device items, but it shows only the most recently accessed items. If you are looking for content that is not visible on the Carousel, use the Navigation menu to access the type of content you're seeking (books, music, and so on), and then download the item you want from that screen.

>>>Go Further

Removing Downloaded Items from Your Kindle Fire

After an item is downloaded, it takes up some of the memory on your Kindle Fire. The amount of memory you have available varies by which model of the Kindle Fire you own. You can free up memory by removing unused items from your device. This removes only the device copy of the item; this content is still available to you in your cloud library, so you can download it again at a later date.

1. Tap and hold the item you want to remove.

2. Tap Remove from Device.

Cloud Versus Device

Cloud is a common buzzword in today's technology. If something is in the cloud, it means that it exists on a computer that you access via the Internet instead of on your local device. The Kindle Fire accesses a lot of its content on Amazon's computers in the cloud.

Many screens on the Kindle Fire enable you to choose whether you are viewing content on the device or in the cloud. Having content in the cloud makes sharing that content among multiple devices easy. You can read the same book or watch the same movie on your Kindle Fire, your computer, and your smartphone.

Adding an Item to Favorites

The Favorites drawer appears below the Carousel when you press the star icon in the lower-right corner. It provides a convenient way for you to access your most-often-used items. You can add any item to Favorites.

1. Tap and hold the item you want to add to Favorites.

2. Tap Add to Favorites.

3. Tap the Favorites icon.

4. Your Favorites appear on shelves below the carousel.

Adding Subscription Items to Favorites

If you add a subscription item to Favorites and that item isn't currently on your device, the item is downloaded immediately. If you remove that item from your device later, it is automatically removed from Favorites as well.

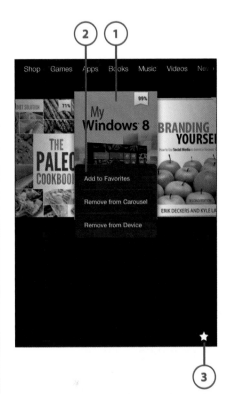

Removing an Item from Favorites

If you decide that you no longer want an item to be listed in Favorites, you can remove it.

1. Tap and hold the item in Favorites.
2. Tap Remove from Favorites.

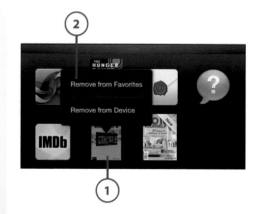

Rearranging Favorites

By default, items are listed in Favorites in the order in which you add them. If you want to rearrange your Favorites, you can easily do so.

1. Tap and hold the item you want to move. Don't lift your finger, even when you see the Remove from Favorites menu pop up.

2. Drag the item to the new location.

3. Release the item.

Changing the Screen Timeout

While you're learning how to use your Kindle Fire, particularly if you are doing each task as you follow along with this book, you might get frustrated if the device automatically goes into sleep mode just as you're about to reach for it. Your Kindle Fire's screen turns off automatically after 5 minutes without use. You can adjust the timeout or completely turn off the automatic timeout.

1. Tap the top of the screen (where the name of the device and time are displayed) and drag down.

2. Tap More.

3. Tap Sounds & Display.

4. Tap Screen Timeout.

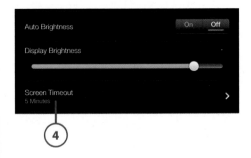

5. Select a screen timeout period.

6. Press the Home button to return to the home screen.

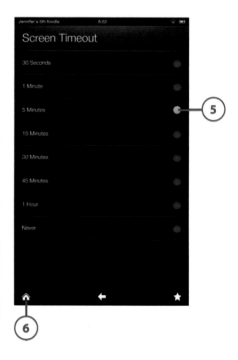

Notifications and Options

The status bar appears at the top of the Kindle Fire screen. It displays the name of your Kindle Fire, a notification indicator (if notifications are present), the clock, the Wi-Fi signal indicator, and the battery meter. If you have the Kindle Fire HD 8.9-inch 4G LTE, the status bar also displays your 4G signal strength.

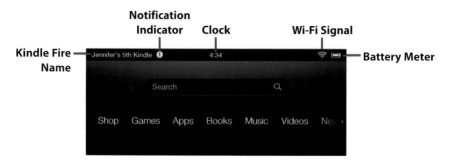

Notifications

Your Kindle Fire uses the notification indicator to inform you of the status of background tasks and let you know when you've received e-mail. When you see the notification indicator, you can tap it to get more information.

1. Swipe the status bar downward to open the notifications.

2. Tap a notification for more information or additional options.

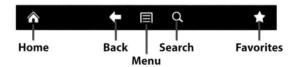

Options

The Options bar appears at the bottom of many screens. The buttons on the Options bar are called icons and include a Home icon, a Back icon, a Menu icon, a Search icon, and the Favorites icon on most screens. The Home icon always takes you to the home screen. The Back icon takes you back one screen, the Menu icon displays a menu for the current screen, the Search icon displays the Search screen, and the Favorites icon opens the Favorites shelf.

Home   Back   Search   Favorites
Menu

Other Options Bar Icons

Depending on the screen, you might see additional icons on the Options bar. These are covered throughout the book, where applicable.

Settings

I cover many of the Kindle Fire's settings throughout the book as necessary, but you should be immediately familiar with some general settings.

Locking the Screen Orientation

Your Kindle Fire features an accelerometer that can sense the orientation of the device. When you turn the device while holding it, the screen rotates automatically to match the orientation of the device. In some cases, you might want to prevent the screen from rotating. For example, if you're reading a web page in portrait mode, setting your Kindle Fire on a table sometimes flips the orientation. You can lock the orientation to prevent this.

Orientation Isn't Always Your Choice

If you are watching videos, your Kindle Fire automatically switches to landscape orientation.

1. With the screen displaying the desired orientation, swipe the status bar down to open the Settings drawer.

2. Tap Unlocked to lock the orientation. The label on the icon changes to Locked.

Adjusting the Volume

A toggle button at the top of the device enables you to adjust the volume. When you press these buttons, a volume meter also appears on the screen to indicate the volume level. You can adjust the volume directly on the screen as well.

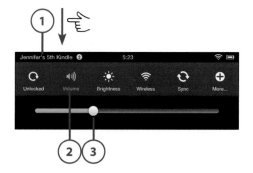

1. Swipe the status bar down to open the Settings drawer.

2. Tap Volume. The volume control appears.

3. Slide the volume control to the right to increase volume and to the left to decrease volume.

It's Not All Good

Using the Volume Toggle Switch

When you are holding your Kindle Fire in portrait mode, the volume toggles at the top of the device are counterintuitive. If you press the button to the right, the volume goes down. If you press the button to the left, the volume increases. Watch the volume control as you use these buttons, to adjust the volume to your liking.

Adjusting Screen Brightness

As mentioned earlier, the screen on the Kindle Fire uses more power than anything else, and the brighter the screen, the more battery power it uses. To increase battery life, you can lower the brightness of the display.

1. Swipe the status bar down to open the Settings drawer.

2. Tap Brightness.

3. Slide the brightness control to the right to increase brightness and to the left to decrease brightness.

Checking Device Information

The Device screen displays information about your Kindle Fire, such as the percentage of battery remaining, how much storage space you've used, the version of your operating system, and other useful information.

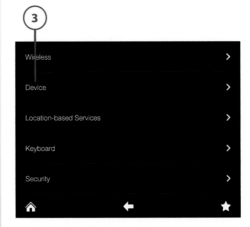

1. Swipe the status bar down to open the Settings drawer.

2. Tap More.

3. Tap Device.

4. The Device screen displays. If you want to check your storage space, tap Storage.

5. The Storage screen displays. Here you can see how much space you have used across various types of data and how much remains available for future use.

Turning Off Wi-Fi

Sometimes you need to turn off the Wi-Fi connection on your Kindle Fire, such as when you're traveling by air or in other sensitive areas. Turning off Wi-Fi also consumes less battery power when you don't need to access online content.

1. Swipe the status bar down to open the Settings drawer.

2. Tap Wireless.

3. Tap Off to turn off Wi-Fi. To reconnect, tap On.

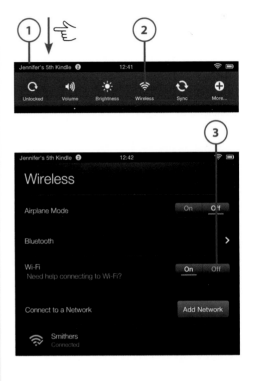

Disconnecting from All Signals

If you are flying on a commercial airline, you will need to turn off Wi-Fi and all other wireless signals on your Kindle Fire, at least during takeoff and landing. Use the On/Off buttons for Airplane Mode on the Wireless screen to disable Wi-Fi, cellular (on the Kindle Fire HD 8.9-inch 4G LTE model), and Bluetooth signals.

Using the Keyboard

Your Kindle Fire's keyboard is much like the keyboard you use on your computer. However, unlike your computer's keyboard, this one has no physical keys. Instead, your Kindle Fire's keyboard uses touch, just like the rest of the interface.

At first, you might find the Kindle Fire's keyboard a bit hard to get used to, especially if you're typing a lengthy e-mail or document. After some time, however, you'll find it to be an easy way to enter data.

Entering Text

Entering text using your Kindle Fire's keyboard is a simple task, and a few convenient features make it easier.

1. Tap an area where text entry is possible, such as an e-mail message.

2. Tap letters on the keyboard to enter your text.

3. Tap a suggested word to insert the word.

A Couple of Shortcuts

You can quickly add a period to the end of a sentence by double-tapping the space key.

You can activate caps lock by double-tapping the Shift key.

Positioning the Cursor

As you type, characters are added at the position of the cursor. You can reposition the cursor, if necessary.

1. Tap in the text entry area.

2. Tap a new position to move the cursor indicator.

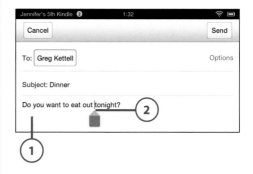

Selecting and Editing Text

If you want to change or remove some of the text you've entered, you can select a block of text instead of deleting one character at a time.

1. Double-tap the entered text.

2. Drag the left indicator to the beginning of your desired selection.

3. Drag the right indicator to the end of your desired selection.

4. Press Backspace to delete the selection or type to replace the selection.

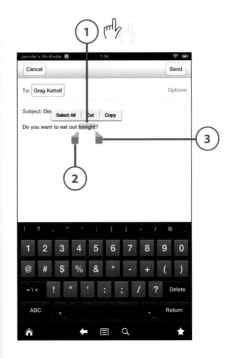

Selecting an Entire Block of Text

If you want to select everything you typed into a text area, such as the entire body of an e-mail message, tap Select All above the selection indicators.

Copying/Cutting and Pasting Text

You might want to copy or cut a selection of text and then paste it somewhere else. You can paste text either within the same message or document or into another message or document.

1. Double-tap the text you want to copy or cut.

2. Drag the indicators to make your selection, or tap Select All.

3. Tap Copy or Cut.

4. Tap and hold where you want to paste the text you copied or cut.

5. Tap Paste.

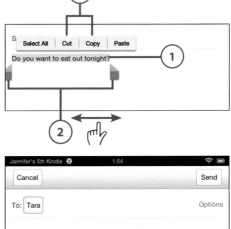

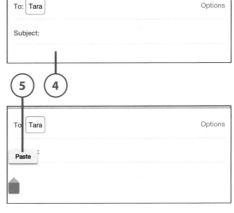

Entering Punctuation and Numbers

The most-often-used punctuation marks appear above the keyboard for easy access while you type. You can use the number keyboard to enter other punctuation, numbers, and symbols.

1. Tap the number key to change the keyboard so that it displays numbers and punctuation marks.

2. Tap the symbols key to change the keyboard so that it displays symbols.

3. Tap a number, punctuation mark, or symbol to enter it.

4. Tap the ABC key to return to the alphabet keyboard.

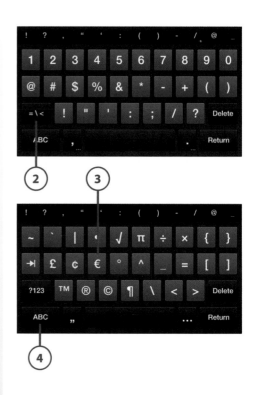

Adding Accent Marks and Diacriticals

If you are typing in a foreign language, you might need to add accent marks and diacriticals to certain letters. The letters that often require these marks are a, e, i, o, u, c, and n.

1. Tap and hold a letter that requires an accent.

2. Without lifting your finger from the keyboard, slide your finger to highlight the desired character and release.

Accessing Hidden Keyboard Features

As with adding accent marks, if you tap and hold the period (.) key, you can quickly slide your finger over additional punctuation marks without having to switch to the number keyboard.

If you tap and hold the comma (,) key and then slide your finger over the symbol that appears, you bring up the Keyboard options.

Connecting to Other Hardware

The Kindle Fire is a self-contained device. You can access your content directly from the Kindle Fire without connecting it to a computer or any other hardware. However, you might want to use accessories that will enhance the quality of your interaction with your Kindle Fire. You can pair the Kindle Fire with Bluetooth keyboards, headphones, or speakers. You can also use an HDMI cable to connect with a television or larger monitor so that you can view your movies on a larger screen.

Adding Bluetooth Accessories

Bluetooth keyboards and headsets can connect wirelessly to your device. With Bluetooth headphones, you can listen to your music without being attached to your Kindle Fire by a wire. A Bluetooth keyboard can help you type messages and documents faster. If you have Bluetooth speakers in your car, you can even play music from your Kindle Fire over your car stereo.

1. Swipe the status bar down to open the Settings drawer.

2. Select Wireless.

3. Select Bluetooth.

4. Tap the On button to enable Bluetooth.

5. After the Kindle Fire locates available devices, tap the device you want to pair with.

6. Follow additional instructions, which vary by device.

t's Not All Good

Bluetooth Has Limits

Although Bluetooth microphones and headsets are popular, particularly among gamers, the Kindle Fire does not support these devices. If you want to use voice chat, you must use the Kindle Fire's built-in microphone.

Go Further

SHARING YOUR SCREEN

The Kindle Fire comes with an HDMI port, located to the left of the mini-USB port. You can use a micro-HDMI-to-HDMI cable to connect to an external display or television. That display will then mirror the display on your Kindle Fire. You do not need to adjust any other settings or go through any menus to make this connection.

Searches

All the content in your Kindle library is indexed for easy searching. Search is more useful than it might seem at first. For example, when you're reading a novel, you can use search to find references to a particular character. This is especially helpful when you pick up a book that you haven't read in a while.

Search results include content both on your device and in the cloud.

Searching Within Content

You can also search within books and other content. I cover how to do that in the "Searching Content and Accessing Reference Materials" section of Chapter 4, "Reading on the Kindle Fire."

Searching Your Library

Searching your library returns results from books, periodicals, music, documents, and apps.

1. From the Home screen, tap inside the search box.

2. Tap Libraries to search your library.

3. Enter the text you want to search for using the keyboard that appears at the bottom of the screen. Results appear as you type.

4. Tap the item you want. If the item is on your device, it opens. If the item is stored on the Amazon cloud, it downloads to your Kindle Fire.

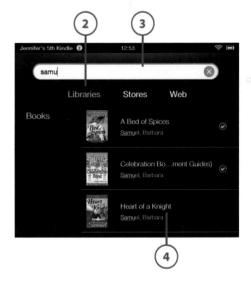

Searching the Web

In addition to searching for items in your libraries, you can search the Web quickly from the home screen.

1. From the home screen, tap inside the search box.

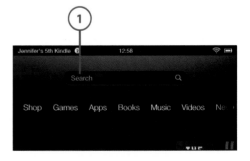

2. Tap Web to search the Web.

3. Enter the text you want to search for. Results appear as you type.

4. Tap an item in the results to open a search page using your default search engine. The preset default search engine is Bing.

Changing Your Web Search Engine

I cover how to set your default web search engine in Chapter 12, "Browsing the Web with Silk."

Searching Amazon Stores

You can search for items in the Amazon Stores from the Home screen. This is similar to performing a search on the Amazon website, but you can do it right from your Kindle Fire.

1. From the home screen, tap inside the search box.

2. Tap Stores to search Amazon Stores.

3. Enter the text you want to search for. Results appear as you type.

4. Tap an option in the results to get a list of items from a particular Amazon Store that match your search terms.

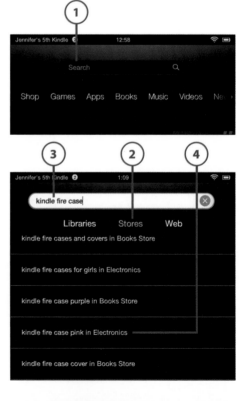

5. Tap the item you want to see from the list of items.

Cloud Player
and Cloud
Drive

Instant
Video

Cloud
Reader

In this chapter, you learn how to load Amazon and other content onto your Kindle Fire and use Amazon's Cloud to access content from your computer. Topics include the following:

→ Amazon Prime

→ Amazon Cloud Drive

→ Amazon Cloud Player

→ Amazon Instant Video

→ Kindle Reader Applications and Kindle Cloud Reader

→ Transferring files from your computer

Loading Your Kindle Fire

Amazon offers a collection of cloud services that augment the functionality of the Kindle Fire. In fact, your Kindle Fire is designed to be a handheld conduit into these cloud services. You can set up a cloud drive, add all your music, and have that music immediately available to you on your Kindle Fire anywhere you can connect to Wi-Fi (or 4G, if you have a Kindle Fire HD 8.9-inch 4G LTE). You can get a movie or TV show from Amazon on your computer or set-top box, watch part of it on your television, and then pick right up to watch the rest on your Kindle Fire while in bed or while traveling. You can also use Amazon's Cloud Services to load your personal photos and documents onto your Kindle Fire. Even if you leave your Kindle Fire behind, all your music, books, videos, and personal files are accessible from any computer with an Internet connection or from many mobile devices.

Amazon Prime

The key to accessing Amazon's Cloud Services is your Amazon account. A standard Amazon account enables you to manage your Kindle Fire device (more on that in Chapter 3, "Using Amazon's Manage Your Kindle Page") and to purchase books, music, and much more. To get the full value out of your Kindle Fire, however, consider upgrading to an Amazon Prime account.

An Amazon Prime account costs $79 per year. For that price, you get the following:

- **Prime Instant Videos:** Unlimited, instant streaming of thousands of movies and television shows, all commercial free. You can watch on your Kindle Fire or on any other Internet-connected TV or game machine you own.

- **Kindle Lending Library:** You can check out one book per month from the Kindle Lending Library catalog without any due dates and load it on your Kindle Fire. The Kindle Lending Library has more than 180,000 titles, so you're sure to find something to read each month.

- **Free two-day shipping:** When you shop for material goods on the Amazon site, you get free two-day shipping on most items. One-day shipping costs only $3.99 per item for eligible purchases. The Amazon Store sells everything from toys, to food, to clothing, so it's easy to see a return on your $79 Prime membership investment if you frequently shop online.

Extended Prime Benefits for Caregivers

If you are the primary caregiver (mom, dad, grandparent, and so forth) of a young child, you can get a 3-month subscription to Prime and 20 percent off diapers and wipes by joining Amazon Mom. Browse to www.amazon.com/prime for details.

Setting Up Amazon Prime

When you went through the setup process for your Kindle Fire, you either connected to an existing Amazon account or created a new one. You can set up a free trial of Prime on the same account. You do this on your Kindle Fire using the Silk browser or via the web browser on your computer.

1. Open a web browser and navigate to www.amazon.com.

2. Click Join Prime. If you are not already logged in to your Amazon account, enter your e-mail address and password.

3. Click Start Your One Month Free Trial.

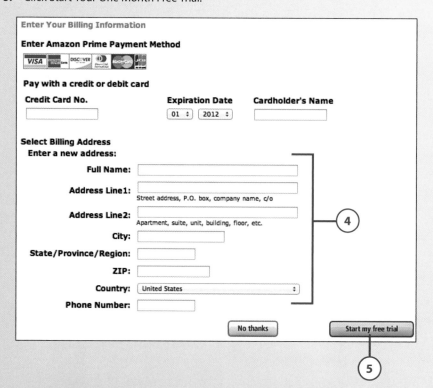

4. Enter your billing information.

5. Select Start My Free Trial.

Prime All the Time

At the end of your free trial, Amazon automatically bills you for $79 to extend your Prime membership for a full year. If you decide that you don't want to keep Prime, go to the Amazon.com site, select Your Account, and then select Do Not Upgrade sometime before the end of your 30-day trial.

Amazon Cloud Drive

Your computer has a hard drive in it where you can store your stuff. When you're sitting at your computer, that stuff is easy to access, but what about when you're not at your computer? The cloud is like having a hard drive available from anywhere you have Internet access.

Amazon provides 5GB of free storage that you can use for photos, personal documents, or anything else you want to store in the cloud. This space is in addition to the unlimited cloud storage Amazon provides for books, music, and videos you purchase directly from Amazon. If you need additional storage, Amazon offers plans from 20GB for $10 a year to 1,000GB for $500 a year. As a frame of reference, a typical HD movie is approximately 2GB. A single song is 3MB to 6MB, while a complete album is around 50MB. A high-quality photo is about 2MB to 3MB. As you see, if you start putting all these items onto your cloud storage, it can fill up quickly.

Go Further

WHY WOULD YOU NEED MORE SPACE?

You can use your Amazon Cloud Drive for more than just making your files accessible to your Kindle Fire. Your Cloud Drive can serve as a backup for important files in case of a crash. You can also use it to access your files from any other computer with Internet access, simply by logging in to your Amazon account.

Content you purchase on Amazon is automatically accessible from your Amazon Cloud account and, thus, from your Kindle Fire. But to access your personal photos and documents, you must upload them to your Cloud Drive.

Upload Files Button

File and Folder Management

Folders   **Amount of Used Storage**

Accessing Your Cloud Drive

You can access your Cloud Drive using Silk on your Kindle Fire or using the web browser on your computer.

1. Open your web browser and go to www.amazon.com.

2. Point to Shop All Departments. If you are using your computer's web browser and have a large enough window open, this menu might already be open when you navigate to the Amazon site.

3. Point to Amazon Cloud Drive.

4. Select Your Cloud Drive from the menu. You might get a prompt to install the desktop application, which I explain later in this chapter. You can install it at this time or click Continue to Your Cloud Drive. (Enter your e-mail address and Amazon password, if prompted.)

After you log in, you'll see your Cloud Drive and a big Upload button to get you started. I show you how to create folders and upload files next.

Creating Folders

By default, your Cloud Drive contains folders for the common file types. You'll see folders for pictures, documents, and videos. Those folders are a good starting point, but you might want to create additional folders. For example, if you're uploading pictures of your pets, you might want to first create a folder inside the Pictures folder called Pets and then upload those pictures there.

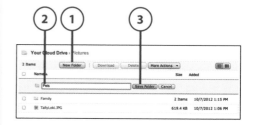

1. Click New Folder. If you want to place the new folder within another folder, first click that folder from the Folders sidebar.

2. Enter a name for the folder.

3. Click Save Folder.

More Actions

You can copy, move, and rename files and folders using the More Actions button.

Deleting Folders

You can delete folders from your Cloud Drive that you no longer need or to free up some space.

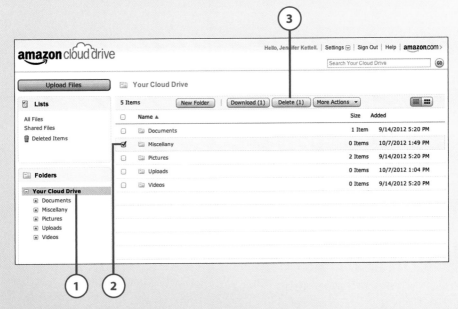

1. Click Your Cloud Drive so that your folders are visible.

2. Check the box to the left of the folder(s) you want to delete.

3. Click Delete. You will not see confirmation of this action, so be sure you choose your files correctly.

Recovering Deleted Items

If you accidentally delete your files, you can recover them. If you delete a folder that contains files, the files are deleted along with the folder. Recovering a folder also recovers the files that were originally inside the folder.

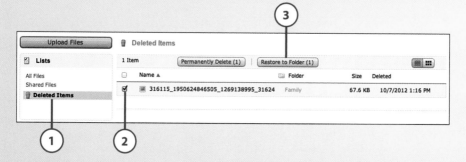

1. Click Deleted Items.
2. Check the box to the left of the files or folders you want to recover.
3. Click Restore to Folder.

Permanently Deleting Files

When you delete a file or folder, it is moved to a Deleted Items folder and continues to use space in your Cloud Drive. To permanently delete these items, click the Permanently Delete button in Deleted Items.

Adding Files to Your Cloud Drive

To add files to your Cloud Drive, you upload them to Amazon.

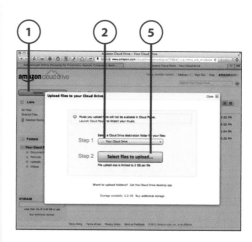

1. Click the Upload Files button near the top-left corner of the Cloud Drive screen.
2. Click the drop-down list to select a folder for your uploaded files.

3. Select your folder.

4. Click Select.

5. Click Select Files to Upload, locate the files on your computer, and select them.

After step 1, you might see a notice about the Amazon Cloud Drive application. You can choose to follow the prompts and download this application or proceed uploading your files using your web browser.

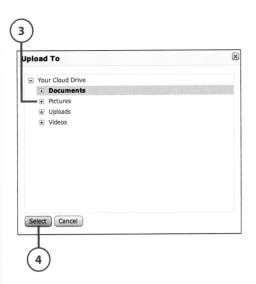

Downloading the Cloud Drive Application

If you use your Cloud Drive on a regular basis, you might find it easier to download and use the Amazon Cloud Drive application. You can download and install it when you see the prompt as you attempt to upload from your web browser, or you can install it at any other time.

1. On your computer, go to www.amazon.com.

2. If the Shop All Departments menu is not already open, hover over it.

3. Point to Amazon Cloud Drive.

4. Click Get the Desktop App.

5. On the page that appears, click Get the Desktop App. The application downloads to your computer. When the download is complete, double-click the file to initiate the installation procedure.

6. Follow the instructions to install the Amazon Cloud Drive application on your computer.

7. Enter your Amazon account username and password.

8. Click Sign In.

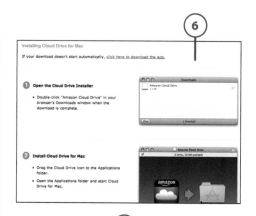

Using the Amazon Cloud Drive Application

After you sign in for the first time, the application provides a few screens with hints on how to get the most out of it. On a Mac, you can either drag files over the Amazon Cloud Drive icon in the menu bar or right-click a file and select Services | Upload to Amazon Cloud Drive (if you're uploading a picture) or simply Upload to Amazon Cloud Drive (if you're uploading a document). On a PC, you can drag files over the Amazon Cloud Drive icon in the taskbar or right-click a file and select Send To | Amazon Cloud Drive.

Accessing Cloud Drive Files from Your Kindle Fire

Your Kindle Fire automatically syncs with your Cloud Drive whenever you have a Wi-Fi connection. Files on your Cloud Drive are automatically sorted into the appropriate content library. If you want to view the photos you uploaded to your Cloud Drive, for example, you can find them in Photos. Personal documents are found in the Docs library.

1. Use the Navigation menu to access the library for the files you want to view. In this example, we access the Docs library.

2. Press the Cloud button if it's not already selected.

3. View a list of the files you have in the cloud for that library.

Folders and Subfolders

Folders and subfolders keep your documents organized. When you view your Docs library By Name, By Recent, or By Type, all of your documents are listed no matter how they're grouped in your Cloud Drive. View your docs By Folder to only see documents within a particular folder or subfolder.

Saving Files to Your Device

When you select a document from the Docs library, it is automatically saved onto your Kindle Fire, and you can then open it from either the Cloud or Device options. The process for transferring photos onto your device is a bit different.

1. Select Photos from the navigation bar.

2. Select a photo or folder from the Cloud library.

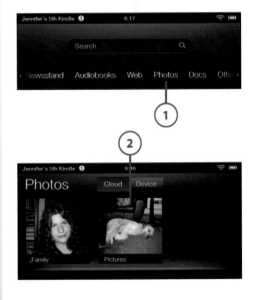

3. Tap the menu button.

4. Select Download.

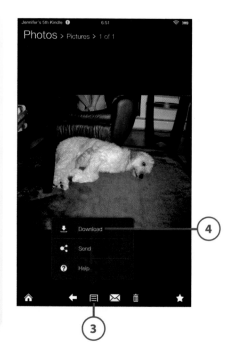

DOWNLOADING FILES FROM YOUR CLOUD DRIVE TO A COMPUTER

You can also download files from your Cloud Drive onto a PC or Mac or even a tablet or smartphone. Use a web browser to navigate to www.amazon.com, and then sign into your account. Access your Cloud Drive, and then check the boxes to the left of the content you want to download. Click Download and select the folder where you want to save the file.

Amazon Cloud Player

Amazon Cloud Player is a convenient way to manage music on your Cloud Drive. You can also use it to listen to your music when you don't have your Kindle Fire with you, because it is available from any computer with Internet access or on most mobile devices.

Your Music   **Album**   **Songs**

Play Controls   **Now Playing**

Launching Cloud Player

You can access Amazon Cloud Player from your web browser.

1. Open your web browser and go to www.amazon.com.

2. Point to MP3s & Cloud Player on the menu.

3. Click Cloud Player for Web. If prompted, enter your e-mail address and Amazon password.

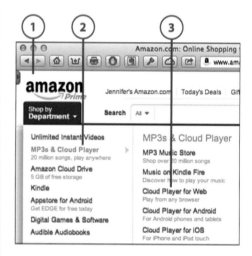

Amazon Cloud Player on the Kindle Fire

Although you can use Silk to access Cloud Player, doing so doesn't make sense. The Music screen on your Kindle Fire provides access to all your Cloud Drive music.

Importing Your Music

You can easily upload your music to Amazon Cloud Player. You can upload up to 250 songs for free or upgrade to a Premium account that stores up to 250,000 songs for $24.99 a year.

1. Open the Amazon Cloud Player.

2. Click Import Your Music.

3. Click the Download Now button to download the Amazon Music Importer application, and follow the installation instructions.

4. Open the Amazon Music Importer application.

5. Authorize your computer by giving the device a name.

6. Click Authorize Device.

7. Click Start Scan. The Amazon Music Importer application scans your hard drive, including your iTunes folders, for music.

8. After the scan is complete, you might be prompted to choose to upgrade to Cloud Player Premium for $24.99 a year or to select up to 250 songs free.

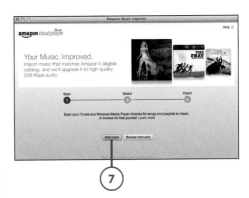

9. To select which songs to import into your Cloud Player, check the boxes to the left of the song, album, artist, or playlist title. You can also choose to import the 250 songs you most recently played on your computer.

10. Click Import Selected.

11. When the import is finished, click Close.

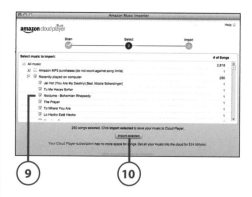

Music that you purchase directly from Amazon's MP3 Store is automatically added to your Amazon Cloud Player. It also does not count against your 250 song or Premium storage limitation.

CONVERTING YOUR MUSIC

The Amazon Cloud Player can import music in either MP3 or unprotected AAC (iTunes) format. If your music is in some other format, you can find free converters by searching the Internet.

>>>Go Further

Playing Music on Your Computer

You can stream music from the Cloud Player without downloading the music to your computer.

1.   Locate the music you want to play. You can browse by song, album, artist, or genre.

2.   Click the check box next to one or more songs to select the songs to play. You can also check the box at the top of the list to select all songs that are displayed.

3.   Click the Play button.

4.   To go to the next song, click the Next button.

5.   To go to the previous song, click the Previous button.

Shuffle and Repeat Songs

You can shuffle or repeat the songs you are playing by clicking the Repeat or Random button under the large Play button in the lower-left corner of Cloud Player.

Creating Playlists

You can create playlists of songs to play only the songs you want to hear. Playlists are a great way to make a song list for a party or special event. Playlists you create in Cloud Player are also available on your Kindle Fire.

1. Select the songs you want to add to your playlist.

2. Click the Add to Playlist button.

3. If you haven't created a playlist, enter a name for a new playlist. Otherwise, choose New Playlist or an existing playlist for the selected songs.

4. Browse to other songs, and add them to your playlist as desired.

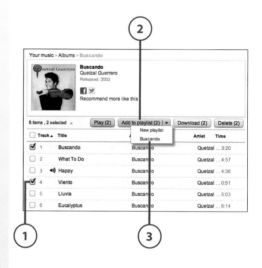

Refreshing Cloud Drive

Your Cloud Drive refreshes on your Kindle Fire every 10 minutes. Songs or playlists that you add appear after a refresh. If you're in a hurry to get your songs or playlists onto your Kindle Fire, swipe down from the status bar on your Kindle Fire to open the Settings drawer, and then choose Sync.

Downloading Songs to Your Kindle Fire

If you plan to be away from an Internet connection, you can still play your music by first downloading it to your Kindle Fire.

1. On the navigation bar of your Kindle Fire, press Music.

2. In the Cloud tab, select a playlist, artist, album, or song.

3. Click the Download All button.

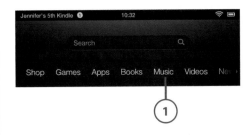

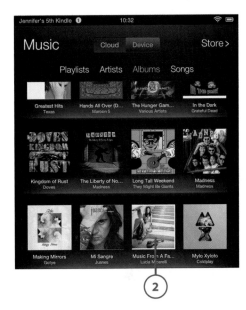

4. If you want to exclude some songs for an artist or album from being downloaded, select the X to the right of the song title. When the download is complete, press Device to confirm that your music is now stored on your Kindle Fire.

Downloading Songs to a Computer

If you want to download your music to a computer, use a web browser to access the Amazon Cloud Player. Select the songs you want to download and then click the Download button. You are prompted to download and install the Amazon MP3 Downloader if it hasn't previously been installed. After the MP3 Downloader is installed, clicking the Download button automatically downloads a link to the selected music to your computer. Double-click the downloaded file, and the MP3 Downloader imports the music into iTunes or Windows Media Player on your computer.

>>>Go Further

CHANGING MP3 DOWNLOADER OPTIONS

The MP3 Downloader detects whether you have iTunes installed. If you do, after it downloads a song, it automatically imports that song into iTunes. This saves you the trouble of importing your music to your iTunes library. If you don't like this behavior, however, you can change it. You can also change the folder where MP3 Downloader saves the songs you download.

To change MP3 Downloader options, click File | Preferences (on a Mac, click Amazon MP3 Downloader | Preferences). You can click the Save Downloads To option to save your songs to a different folder. You can also deselect the check box Add Downloaded Tracks to iTunes.

Changing these settings is best done before you start downloading songs. You can find the MP3 Downloader on your PC in the Amazon folder on your Start menu. On the Mac, you can locate it in your Applications folder.

Changing How Amazon Handles Purchased Music

You can choose whether Amazon automatically downloads your purchased music to your computer.

1. Click Settings from the Amazon Cloud Player.

2. Select Your Amazon MP3 Settings. Enter your e-mail address and password, if prompted.

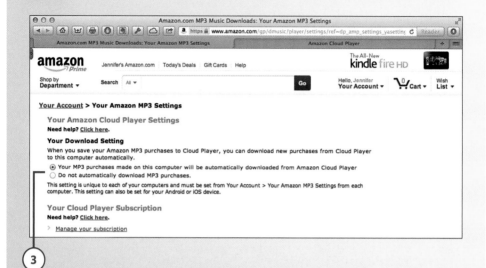

3. Choose whether music added to your Cloud Drive should be downloaded to your computer.

   This setting is computer dependent, not linked to your Amazon account. If you access your Amazon account from multiple computers, you need to change this setting on each computer.

Amazon Instant Video

Amazon has a huge selection of videos, including both movies and television programs, that you can watch on your Kindle Fire. You can also watch those videos on your computer. You can even purchase or rent videos on your computer and watch them on your Kindle Fire, or vice versa.

Getting Videos from Amazon Instant Video

You can use your computer to buy, rent, or stream Amazon Instant Video. Videos that you buy or rent are available on your computer, on your Kindle Fire, or on any other device that supports Amazon Instant Video.

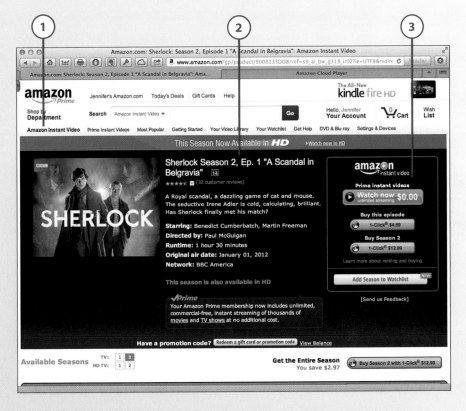

1. Open your web browser and go to www.amazon.com/instantvideo. Or go to www.amazon.com and select Amazon Instant Video from the Shop by Department menu.

2. Select the movie or TV show that you want to watch.

3. Choose to purchase, rent, or watch your video. Not all options are available for all titles.

Choosing HD Movies

If you have one of the HD models of the Kindle Fire, you can choose to watch movies and TV shows in high definition. These are designated with a blue HD band when you choose a video. Videos that are available in multiple formats have links to access the other formats.

>>>Go Further

WHY RENT OR BUY INSTEAD OF STREAM FREE PRIME VIDEO?

If you're an Amazon Prime member, you might be able to watch a title free, but you still might want to rent it instead. Why? If you want to watch on your Kindle Fire and you don't have Wi-Fi access, such as on a long car trip, you need to first download the movie or TV show. You can download only videos that you've either purchased or rented.

If you rent a video, you have 30 days to begin watching it before it expires. After you begin watching it, you have 48 hours to complete it before the rental expires.

Kindle Reader Applications and Kindle Cloud Reader

In addition to reading on your Kindle Fire, Amazon offers free Kindle Reading apps for the PC, the Mac, and most mobile and tablet devices. All these applications enable you to access your Kindle books from the Amazon Cloud and save them to your computer or device to read offline. You can also access your Kindle books from the Kindle Cloud Reader on the Internet.

Accessing Kindle Reader Applications

Before you can read Kindle books on your computer, tablet, or smartphone, you must download and install the appropriate app.

1. In a web browser, go to www.amazon.com.

2. In the Shop By Department menu, choose Kindle, and then choose Free Kindle Reading Apps.

3. Select your computer or device and follow the directions for downloading and installing the appropriate app.

Downloading Smartphone and Tablet Apps

The information pages for each of the smartphone and tablet apps (iPhone and iPod Touch, Android, Windows Phone, BlackBerry, iPad, and Android Tablet) have links to the appropriate store or marketplace to download the required application.

Accessing Kindle Cloud Reader

The Kindle Cloud Reader makes it possible to read your Kindle books in your web browser from any location with Internet access. Kindle Cloud Reader requires a current version of either Google Chrome (www.google.com/chrome), Apple Safari (www.apple.com/safari), or Firefox (www.getfirefox.com).

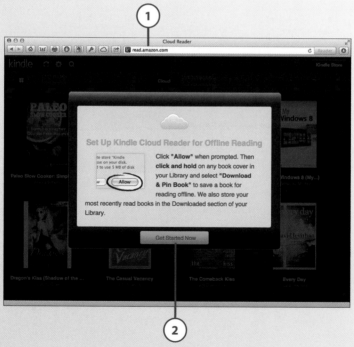

1. Browse to read.amazon.com using your web browser. You can also go to www.amazon.com, choose Kindle from the Shop by Department menu, and then select Kindle Cloud Reader.

2. Click the Get Started Now button.

3. Enter your e-mail address and Amazon password, if prompted.

Cloud button shows books in the Cloud

Downloaded button shows books you've downloaded to your computer

4. View your Kindle Library in your browser window.

Opening and Downloading Books

When you select a book, the Kindle Reader apps or Amazon Cloud Reader automatically begin downloading it to your device or computer. This makes the book available even if you continue reading offline.

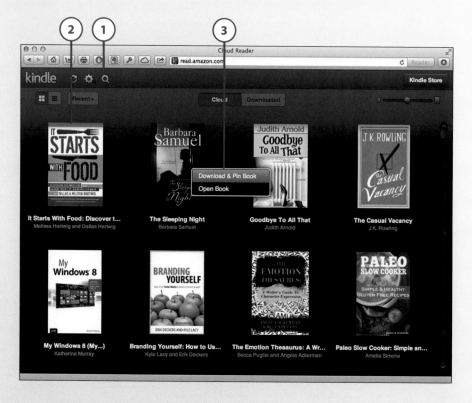

1. Locate the book you want to read. You can click the magnifying glass at the top of the screen to search for books, if necessary.

2. Click a book to start reading it. If you are using the Kindle Cloud Reader, the book begins downloading to your computer as you read. If you are using one of the other Kindle Reader apps, the book downloads to your device and then allows you to read it.

3. If you want to download a book without immediately beginning to read in the Kindle Cloud Reader and computer Kindle Reader apps, right-click the book and click Download & Pin book. In the smartphone Kindle Reader apps, press and hold the book until a Download button appears; then press that button.

Reading Books on the Kindle Cloud Reader

The Kindle Cloud Reader has many features to make reading a book more enjoyable. The other Kindle Reader applications are similar but might have slight differences in the location and method for accessing some features.

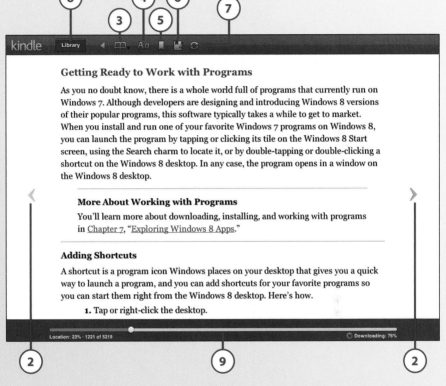

1. Open a book as described in the previous section. If the book has been opened previously on any Kindle device, it automatically opens at the farthest point read.

2. To turn pages, use the arrow keys on your keyboard or click the arrows on the left and right sides of the page.

3. Quickly access a part of the book using the Go To menu.

4. Change font size, margins, and color settings using the View Settings button.

5. Bookmark a page using the Bookmark button.

6. View notes and highlights using the Show Notes and Marks button.

7. Synchronize with your other Kindle devices using the Synchronize button.

8. Click the Library button to return to your library.

9. See where you are in the book using the location bar.

Getting Ready to Work with Programs

As you no doubt know, there is a whole world full of programs that currently run on Windows 7. Although developers are designing and introducing Windows 8 versions of their popular programs, this software typically takes a while to get to market. When you install and run one of your favorite Windows 7 programs on Windows 8, you can launch the program by tapping or clicking its tile on the Windows 8 Start screen, using the Search charm to locate it, or by double-tapping or double-clicking a shortcut on the Windows 8 desktop. In any case, the program opens in a window on the Windows 8 desktop.

Highlight   Note

More About Working with Programs

You'll learn more about downloading, installing, and working with programs in Chapter 7, "Exploring Windows 8 Apps."

(10)

10. To add Notes or Highlights, use your mouse to select the passage you want to mark; then right-click and choose to create a Note or Highlight.

Transferring Files from Your Computer

Most of the content you view on your Kindle Fire is available directly from Amazon and can be easily accessed from the Amazon Cloud. You can also transfer books, videos, music, and other files from other online sources or your personal library. This is known as *sideloading*. To get this content onto your Kindle Fire, transfer the files via the micro-USB cable that came with your device.

Kindle File Types

You can transfer the following types of files onto your Kindle Fire:

- **Books and documents:** AZW, TXT, PDF, MOBI, PRC, DOC, and DOCX formats

- **Audio (Music):** MP3, Non-DRM AAC (.m4a), MIDI, OGG, and WAV formats

- **Video:** MP4 format

- **Images:** JPEG, GIF, PNG, and BMP formats

The Kindle Fire cannot read Mobipocket files that utilize Digital Rights Management (DRM) protection. The Kindle Fire also does not support EPUB books. If you want to read EPUB books on your Kindle Fire, you must convert them to another format and then sideload them. You can find information about this in Chapter 5, "Managing Content with Calibre."

Transferring Files from a PC

If you're using Windows Vista or later, the Kindle Fire automatically shows up as an available external USB drive.

1. Connect your Kindle Fire to your PC using the micro-USB cable.

2. In Windows Explorer, click Computer.

3. Click Kindle.

4. Double-click Internal Storage.

5. Copy your files from their original location on your PC into the appropriate folders in the Internal Storage folder.

Using Windows XP

If you're using Windows XP, you need to update Windows Media Player to transfer files to your Kindle Fire. Windows Media Player 11 for Windows XP is located at www.microsoft.com/en-us/download/details.aspx?id=8163.

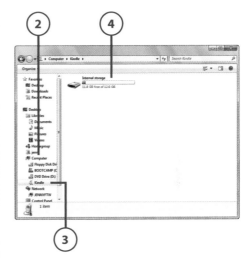

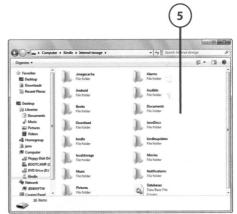

Transferring Files from a Mac

If you're using a Mac, you must download Android File Transfer, a free app, before you can transfer files using USB.

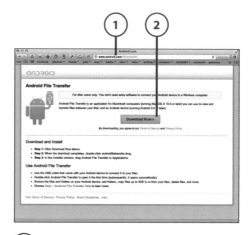

1. In your web browser, go to www.android.com/filetransfer.

2. Click the Download Now button, and follow the instructions to install Android File Transfer to your Applications folder.

3. Use the micro-USB cable to connect your Kindle Fire to your Mac.

4. Double-click the Android File Transfer app to open it. After you've opened it for the first time, it automatically opens whenever you connect your Kindle Fire to your Mac.

5. Copy your files from their original location on your Mac into the appropriate folders in the Android File Transfer app.

>>>Go Further

TRANSFERRING FILES FROM LINUX

If you're a Linux user, you can transfer files to your Kindle Fire using a Media Transfer Protocol (MTP) USB driver. You can find more information about connecting your device using MTP at http://research.jacquette.com/jmtpfs-exchanging-files-between-android-devices-and-linux/.

Manage Content

Manage Devices

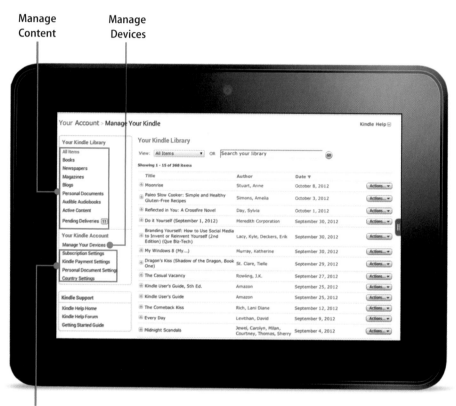

Manage Your Account

In this chapter, you learn how you can use Amazon's Manage Your Kindle page to keep track of your books and subscriptions, and manage your payment and device information. Topics include the following:

→ Managing your books and docs
→ Managing subscriptions
→ Updating Kindle payment information
→ Managing your Kindle devices

Using Amazon's Manage Your Kindle Page

Amazon's Manage Your Kindle page is a one-stop location for managing your Kindle content and your Kindle device. If you have multiple Kindle devices, the Manage Your Kindle Page is even more useful.

You can use the Manage Your Kindle page to send books from your Kindle library to any of your Kindle devices. You can also use it to see the periodicals you subscribe to, and you can manage those subscriptions as well. Links enable you to manage your method of payment to Amazon so that items you purchase on your Kindle Fire get charged to the right credit card. Finally, you can register and deregister Kindles and rename your devices from the Manage Your Kindle page.

Managing Your Books and Docs

You can view all the books and docs in your library using Manage Your Kindle. You can also transfer them to your Kindle. Books are eBooks that you have purchased from Amazon's Kindle store. Your docs can also be eBooks that you purchased from a source other than Amazon. Docs that you see listed in Manage Your Kindle have been e-mailed to your kindle.com e-mail address for document conversion. Manage Your Kindle doesn't list docs that you load to your Kindle Fire using the micro-USB cable (a process known as *sideloading*).

What's Up with Docs?

When I talk about "docs," I'm talking about Kindle Personal Documents. I use the term *docs* because the Kindle Fire uses the Docs screen for your Personal Documents.

Chapter 11, "Managing Your Personal Documents and Data," covers docs in detail.

Accessing Manage Your Kindle

Manage Your Kindle is a web page that you access using the web browser on your computer or using Silk on your Kindle Fire.

1. In your web browser, go to www.amazon.com.
2. Hover over the Your Account drop-down menu.
3. Choose Manage Your Kindle. If prompted, log in using your e-mail address and Amazon password.

A Faster Way to Manage Your Kindle

You can get to the Manage Your Kindle page directly by going to www.amazon.com/manageyourkindle in your web browser.

Viewing Books and Docs

Manage Your Kindle's default view lists your Kindle books, but you can view other content types as well. I talk about handling newspapers and magazines in the next section. This section covers just books and docs.

From the Manage Your Kindle page, you can select the type of content you want to view using the View drop-down list. You can sort content by title, author, or date by clicking one of the column headers. The first click of a column header sorts in descending order; clicking the same column header again sorts that column in ascending order.

If you want to see details on an item, click the plus sign next to the item title. If you have a lot of content and you want to search for a particular item, enter a search term and click Go.

Select the type of content you want to see from the View drop-down.

Search for an item by entering a search term.

Click a column header to order the list.

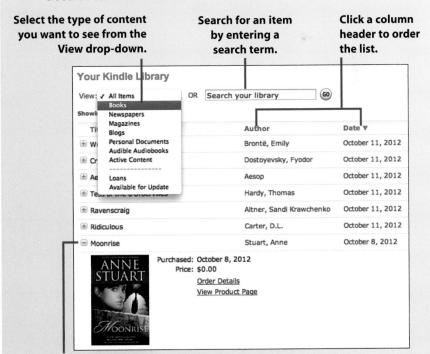

View item details by clicking the plus sign next to the title.

Why Use Manage Your Kindle?

A lot of the functionality in Manage Your Kindle, such as transferring a book from the Amazon cloud to your device, can be accomplished directly on your Kindle Fire. However, if you want to lend a book to another Kindle user, permanently delete a book from your Kindle Library, or deliver a book to another Kindle device, you accomplish those tasks through Manage Your Kindle. It's also a convenient way to manage content on multiple Kindle devices or to manage your account when someone else in the family is using your Kindle Fire.

Sending Books and Docs to Your Kindle

You can send books and docs to a Kindle device or to the Kindle apps for Android, iPad, iPhone, and iPod Touch. You can send books, but not docs, to the other Kindle apps. Content is delivered within a minute, assuming you are connected to Wi-Fi.

Kindle Apps

When I mention Kindle apps in this chapter, I'm not talking about apps installed on your Kindle Fire. I'm talking about the Kindle app that you can use on a computer, tablet, or smartphone to read Kindle eBooks.

1. Locate the book or doc that you want to send to your Kindle.

2. Point to the Actions drop-down list.

3. Click Deliver to My.

4. Select the device from the drop-down list. If the doc you are sending to your Kindle isn't in a format supported by a particular device, that device is not available in the drop-down list.

5. Click Deliver.

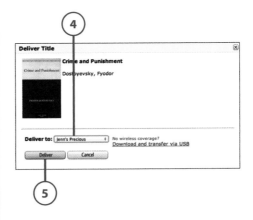

Downloading Books to a Computer

You can also download books (but not docs) to your computer. After you download a book, you can side-load it to your Kindle Fire using the micro-USB cable.

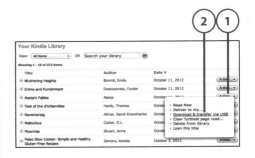

1. Point to the Actions drop-down list.

2. Click Download & Transfer via USB.

3. Select the Kindle to which you plan to transfer the book.

4. Click Download and save the book using your browser's download option.

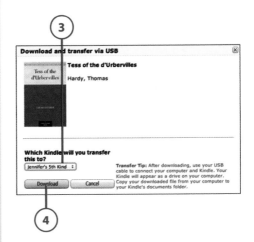

>>>Go Further

WHEN TO DOWNLOAD TO A COMPUTER

If you do not have access to Wi-Fi (or 4G) at home, you can still get content onto your Kindle Fire via USB. If you have a laptop, you can connect to Wi-Fi at a coffeeshop or library and follow the procedure just described to download books to your computer. Your books are then available for you to transfer onto your Kindle Fire via the micro-USB cable at your convenience. You can also sign onto a public computer at an Internet cafe or library, store the books on a flash drive, and then copy them onto your home computer. Transfer the books onto your Kindle Fire using the methods described in the "Transferring Files from Your Computer" section of Chapter 2, "Loading Your Kindle Fire."

Deleting Books and Docs

You can delete books and docs from your library if you do not want to reread them. Use this feature with caution because doing so removes the item permanently. If you delete a book that you purchased from Amazon, you have to buy it again if you change your mind.

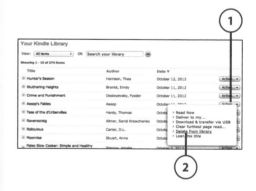

1. Point to the Actions drop-down list.

2. Click Delete from Library.

3. Click Yes to confirm that you want to permanently delete the book from your library.

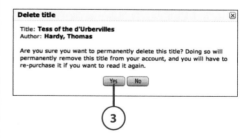

Changing Your Kindle E-mail Address

Use your Kindle e-mail address to send docs directly to your Kindle. You can change the e-mail address for your Kindle Fire on the Manage Your Kindle page.

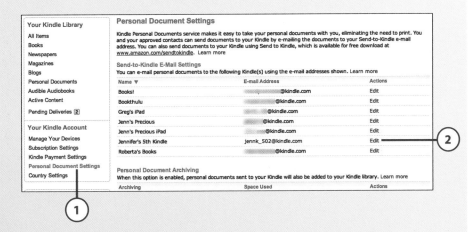

1. Click Personal Document Settings.
2. Click Edit next to the Kindle e-mail address you want to change.

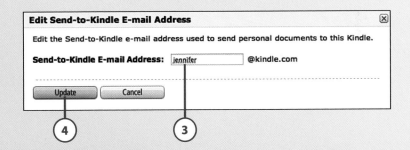

3. Enter the new e-mail address.
4. Click Update.

Adding an Approved E-mail for Docs

To prevent spam on your Kindle device, Amazon delivers only docs e-mailed from an approved list of senders. You can add an approved e-mail address using Personal Documents Settings.

1. From Personal Documents Settings, click Add a New Approved E-mail Address in the Approved Personal Document E-mail List section.

2. Enter the e-mail address you want to approve. You can also enter a partial e-mail address, such as *yourcompany*.com, to allow all senders from that particular domain.

3. Click Add Address.

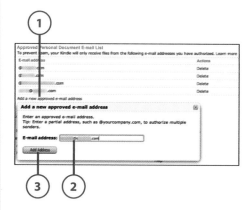

Deleting an Approved E-mail Address

You can delete an approved e-mail address by clicking Delete to the right of the e-mail address on the Approved Personal Document E-mail List.

PUTTING YOUR KINDLE E-MAIL ADDRESS TO WORK

Go Further

Some non-Amazon online bookstores, such as www.fictionwise.com, deliver purchases directly to your Kindle account if you provide them with your Kindle e-mail address. Be sure to add these providers to your approved e-mail list and follow the bookstore site's instructions about adding your Kindle address to your bookstore account before making a purchase.

Disabling Doc Archiving

By default, docs that are sent to your Kindle are also saved in your Kindle library. Amazon gives you 5GB of space for personal doc archiving. You can disable the archiving of personal docs.

1. From Personal Document Settings, click Edit in the Personal Document Archiving section.

2. Deselect the box to disable archiving.

3. Click Update.

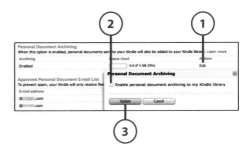

Double the Docs Space

The 5GB of personal doc storage in your Kindle library is separate from the 5GB of storage on your Amazon Cloud Drive, which you can also use for docs (among other files). I recommend saving the Kindle personal doc space for eBook purchases from other bookstores because it is e-mail accessible and using your Amazon Cloud Drive to store your other personal documents. This has the added benefit of keeping all your truly personal docs together on the Amazon Cloud Drive, which makes them easier to manage and organize.

Managing Subscriptions

You can also manage your subscriptions from the Manage Your Kindle page. You can choose which device gets your subscription automatically, send past issues to your Kindle Fire, or download past issues so that you can sideload them to your Kindle Fire. Finally, you can cancel your subscription altogether.

Changing Where a Subscription Is Delivered

You choose which device receives the automatic delivery of subscription content when you first subscribe. If you subscribe from your Kindle Fire, it automatically receives the subscription. You can change that choice from Manage Your Kindle. This option is available only if you have multiple Kindle devices registered.

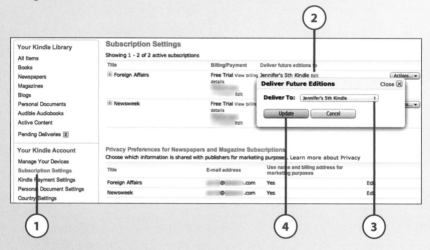

1. Click Subscription Settings.

2. Click Edit for the subscription you want to change.

3. Select a device to which new editions should be delivered.

4. Click Update.

Canceling a Subscription

Subscriptions are automatically charged on a monthly basis, even if the magazine arrives on your Kindle Fire on a different distribution schedule. If you want to cancel a subscription, you can do it from Manage Your Kindle.

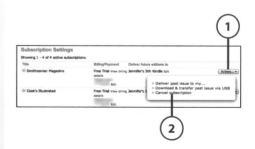

1. From Subscription Settings, click Actions for the subscription you want to cancel.

2. Click Cancel Subscription.

3. Select one or more reasons for canceling.

4. Enter a comment if you select Other.

5. Click Cancel Subscription.

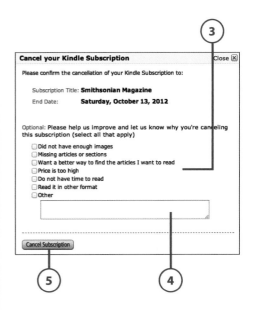

Access to Past Issues for Canceled Subscriptions

If you cancel a subscription, any issues that have been downloaded to your Kindle Fire remain in your library. However, you won't be able to download any past issues. Be sure you've downloaded all the issues for which you've paid before you cancel.

Reactivating a Canceled Subscription

Amazon maintains a list of all your inactive subscriptions. You can use this list to easily reactivate a canceled subscription.

1. From Subscription Settings, click View Inactive Subscriptions.

2. Clilck Actions for the subscription you want to reactivate.

3. Click Reactivate Subscription.

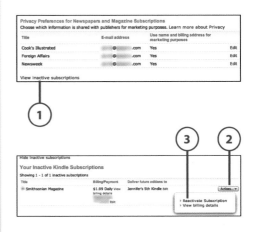

4. Click Reactivate Subscription in the confirmation dialog box.

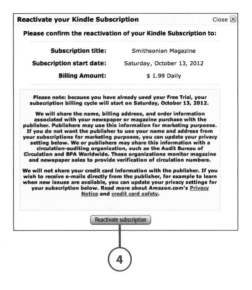

Reactivate your Kindle Subscription   Close ⊠

Please confirm the reactivation of your Kindle Subscription to:

Subscription title: Smithsonian Magazine
Subscription start date: Saturday, October 13, 2012
Billing Amount: $ 1.99 Daily

Please note: because you have already used your Free Trial, your subscription billing cycle will start on Saturday, October 13, 2012.

We will share the name, billing address, and order information associated with your newspaper or magazine purchase with the publisher. Publishers may use this information for marketing purposes. If you do not want the publisher to use your name and address from your subscriptions for marketing purposes, you can update your privacy setting below. We or publishers may share this information with a circulation-auditing organization, such as the Audit Bureau of Circulation and BPA Worldwide. These organizations monitor magazine and newspaper sales to provide verification of circulation numbers.

We will not share your credit card information with the publisher. If you wish to receive e-mails directly from the publisher, for example to learn when new issues are available, you can update your privacy settings for your subscription below. Read more about Amazon.com's Privacy Notice and credit card safety.

[Reactivate subscription]

④

Why Is the Actions Button Missing?

If you have deregistered the Kindle to which an active subscription was being delivered, the Actions button is missing. Before you can reactivate the subscription, you first need to select a Kindle to which the subscription should be delivered.

It's Not All Good

Resubscribing During the Free Trial

Subscriptions typically begin with a free trial period, during which you receive one or more issues. If you do nothing after the free trial, you are automatically billed the monthly rate. If you cancel a subscription during the free trial and then resubscribe, however, you are billed immediately.

Changing Subscription Privacy Settings

Amazon does not share your e-mail address with content providers unless you explicitly give permission to do so. You can do that using subscription privacy settings.

1. From Subscription Settings, locate Privacy Preferences for Newspapers and Magazine Subscriptions.

2. Click Edit for the subscription you want to modify.

3. Check the box(es) for the information you want to share with the content provider.

4. If you want your settings to be the default for future subscriptions, check the appropriate box.

5. Click Update.

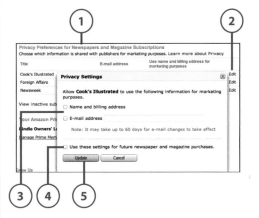

Updating Kindle Payment Information

You can change the credit card that Amazon uses for purchases and for current subscriptions.

Changing Amazon Purchases Credit Cards

When you buy Kindle books and MP3s, and rent or purchase Amazon videos, the credit card used for 1-Click purchases at Amazon.com is billed automatically. You can change this credit card information, add a new credit card, or choose a different credit card using Manage Your Kindle.

Multiple Credit Cards

Amazon can store several cards for your account, and you can choose which one is used for your 1-Click purchases on the Manage Your Kindle page. Keep in mind that changing your credit card does not change the credit card used for your subscriptions; you must change those separately.

1. Click Kindle Payment Settings.

2. Click Edit.

3. Enter your new credit card information, or select a different card.

4. Click Continue.

Changing Current Subscriptions Credit Cards

You must individually update payment options for current subscriptions.

1. From Kindle Payment Settings, click Edit Payment for the subscription you want to change.

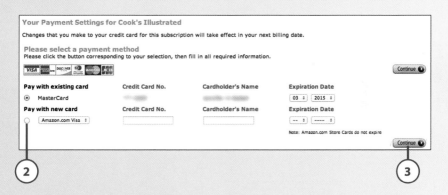

2. Enter the new credit card information.
3. Click Continue.

It's Not All Good

Updating Credit Card Information

Whenever you change your payment information, you need to remember to update each of your subscriptions as well. If you have multiple subscriptions, this can be a time-consuming process, and one easily forgotten when you change your 1-Click account.

Managing Your Kindle Devices

You can add multiple Kindles to your account. Having two or more Kindles registered to the same account is useful if you and other family members have the same tastes in books. If you buy a book on one Kindle, you can read it on another Kindle at the same time without having to buy it again.

The Manage Your Devices page lists all your Kindle devices (including the Kindle app installed on your computer, tablet, or phone). You can deregister a Kindle or change your Kindle's name.

It's Not All Good

Registering a Kindle at Amazon.com

You can also register a new Kindle from the Manage Your Kindle page, but to do so, you need the serial number of the Kindle you're registering. You can't find the serial number for a Kindle Fire without first starting the device and going through the initial setup, part of which is registering the device with Amazon. Therefore, it doesn't make sense to use the Manage Your Kindle page to register a Kindle Fire.

Deregistering a Kindle

If you decide to give away or sell your Kindle Fire, you should deregister it first. This removes the Kindle Fire's access to your account and prevents the new owner from using your credit card information.

1. From the Manage Your Kindle page, click Manage Your Devices.

2. Locate the Kindle you want to deregister and click Deregister.

3. Click the Deregister button.

Renaming Your Kindle Fire

You can change the name of your Kindle device to make it unique and distinguish it from your other Kindles.

1. From Manage Your Devices, locate the Kindle whose name you want to change.

2. Click Edit next to the existing name.

3. Enter a new name for your Kindle.

4. Click Update.

Naming Your Kindle Fire
The name of your device appears on the Kindle Fire home screen. Unless you want to stare at something like "Jennifer's 2nd Kindle" every day, you might want to change it.

Deregistering a Kindle App

You can also deregister a Kindle app on your computer, tablet, or mobile phone.

1. From Manage Your Devices, locate the Registered Kindle Reading Apps section.
2. Click Deregister for the app you want to deregister.
3. Click the Deregister button.

Why Deregister an App?

If your computer, tablet, or mobile phone is lost or stolen, or if you sell or give it away, you should deregister the Kindle app. That way, no purchases can be made against your account without your knowledge.

Turning Off Whispersync

Whispersync keeps all your devices and Kindle apps synchronized. It synchronizes your reading position, notes, highlights, and more. If you personally use multiple devices or apps when reading a book, you might want to keep Whispersync turned on. If multiple people in your home read Kindles registered to the same account, disable Whispersync so that each device can maintain unique page positions, highlights, and notes for a book.

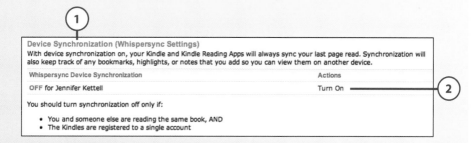

1. In Manage Your Devices, locate the Device Synchronization section.
2. Click Turn Off or Turn On to toggle Whispersync. This change takes effect immediately.

Turning Off Special Offers

Your Kindle Fire displays special offers, ads that appear on the screensaver, at the bottom of the screen, and in the Offers heading of the Navigation bar. You can pay a one-time fee to remove these offers.

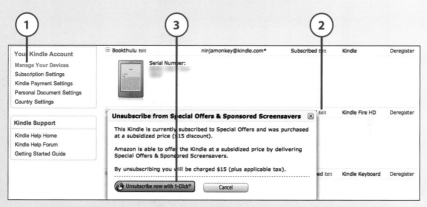

1. In Manage Your Devices, locate the device you want to unsubscribe from special offers.
2. Click Edit in the Special Offers column.
3. Click Unsubscribe Now with 1-Click. Your account is charged $15 to unsubscribe a Kindle Fire from these offers. The cost to unsubscribe other Kindle Devices varies.

Why Should I Have to Pay?

Amazon charges advertising fees for special offers, which they claim subsidizes the cost of the Kindle Fire. Thus, if you opt out, their rationale is that they expect you to pay the projected difference in cost. Many people are not disturbed by the placement of the offers, so I advise you to use your Kindle Fire for a while to see whether removing them is worth the additional cost.

View
Notes &
Bookmarks

Change Display
Settings

Go To a Page
or Location

Learn More
About the Book

Set
Bookmarks

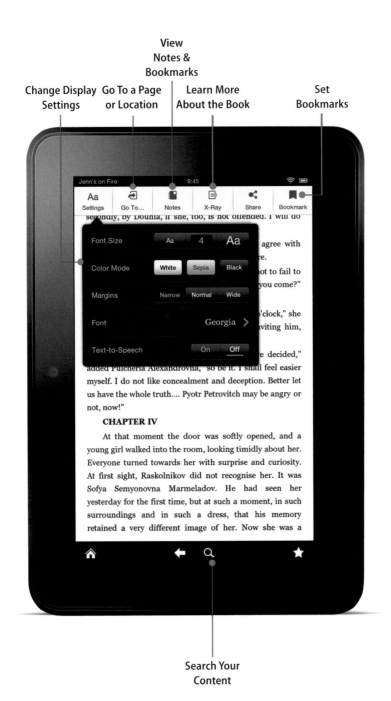

Search Your
Content

In this chapter, you learn about ways that you can find content for your Kindle Fire and how to read and interact with that content. You also discover how you can search your Kindle Fire libraries.

4

→ Finding content
→ Organizing your books
→ Reading on your Kindle
→ Working with notes and highlights
→ Working with bookmarks
→ Reading magazines and newspapers
→ Listening to audiobooks
→ Searching content and accessing reference materials

Reading on the Kindle Fire

Your Kindle Fire is a great tablet computer, but it's still a Kindle eBook reader at heart. Its size makes it convenient to carry with you so that you can read your books, magazines, newspapers, and other content no matter where you are. When it's inconvenient for you to look at the page, the Kindle Fire's audiobook immersion and text-to-speech features can even read for you.

Finding Content

Amazon's Kindle Store provides access to a huge assortment of reading content for your Kindle Fire. You can find just about any book you want to read for the Kindle. In addition to books, Amazon offers a wide array of newspapers and magazines. Because your Kindle Fire's screen is full color, reading periodicals can provide a similar experience to reading a glossy magazine. Reading has also become an auditory experience as much as a visual one, and your Kindle Fire can play audiobooks. If you have both the eBook and audiobook copies of a title, you can immerse yourself in the reading experience, following along with the professional narration, and keep both books in sync.

Your source of great content doesn't stop with Amazon. You can also check out books from your local library, borrow books from friends and family, and even download books from other online eBook stores and websites, and then transfer them to your Kindle Fire.

Accessing Non-Amazon Books

Many other online bookstores deliver your books using your Kindle's e-mail address and the personal document delivery system. You can read more about setting up a unique Kindle e-mail address in Chapter 3, "Using Amazon's Manage Your Kindle Page," and about personal documents in Chapter 11, "Managing Your Personal Documents and Data."

Buying Books

Amazon's Kindle Store has more than 1 million books available for your Kindle Fire.

1. From the Home screen, tap Books.

2. Tap Store.

3. Tap a book that you want to read on your Kindle Fire. View books recommended by Amazon based on previous purchases, current bestsellers, or category.

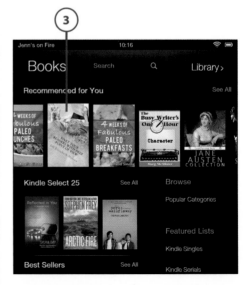

4. If you're trying out a new author or genre, download a free sample first. A free sample is generally the first chapter of a book, sometimes along with the table of contents and other introductory material.

5. Tap Buy to purchase the book and add it to your Kindle library.

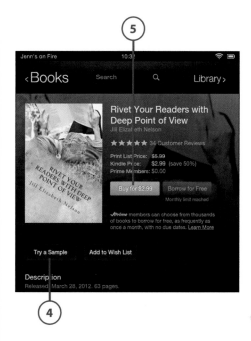

Purchasing After Sampling

If you want to try out a new author or genre, download a free sample first. The length of samples varies based on the book. You can purchase the book if you want to continue reading.

1. At the end of the sample, click Buy Now.

2. Click the Buy button.

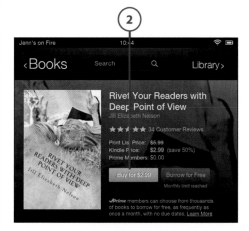

Using the Kindle Lending Library

If you are a Prime subscriber, you can borrow one book per month from the approximately 5,000 books in Amazon's Kindle Owners' Lending Library. You can keep borrowed books as long as you want, but you can borrow only one book in a calendar month.

Check Out Your Local Library

You can also check out Kindle books from thousands of local libraries. To find out if your local library offers this service, go to www.overdrive.com and enter your ZIP Code.

1. From the Home screen, tap Books.

2. Tap Store to open the Kindle Store and locate a book.

3. Locate a book. You can tap Kindle Owners' Lending Library to see a complete list of available titles.

4. If a book is available for borrowing, tap Borrow for Free to borrow the book and add it to your library.

Can't Borrow?

If a book is not available for borrowing, the Borrow for Free button isn't visible. If you've already borrowed a book during the past month, the Borrow for Free button is grayed out.

Only on Kindle Devices

You can borrow or read books from the Kindle Lending Library only on a Kindle device; you cannot borrow or read them from your web browser or any other Kindle app.

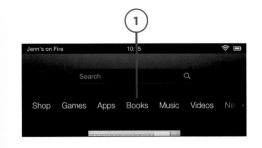

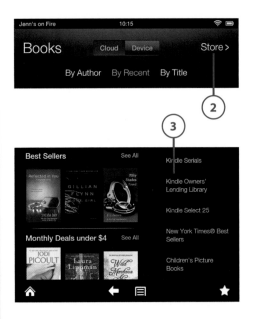

Lending Books to Friends and Family

You can loan some books to friends or family. Your friend or family member isn't required to have a Kindle device to read the book you lend. Loaned books can be read on a computer or other device with the free Kindle application.

1. Open your web browser and go to www.amazon.com/ manageyourkindle.

2. Hover your mouse pointer over the Actions drop-down next to the title you want to lend.

3. Click Loan This Title.

4. Enter your friend or family member's information and a personal message.

5. Click Send Now.

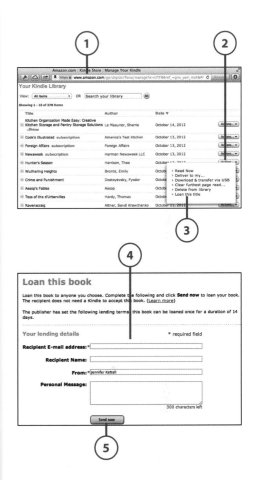

What Happens Next?

When you lend a book, the recipient of the book receives an e-mail with a link to accept the request. That person needs an Amazon account to accept and access the book.

Books are loaned for 14 days, and you will not be able to read the book while it is loaned out to someone. You can see the status of the loan on the Manage Your Kindle page.

It's Not All Good

Why Can't I Lend My Book?

The publisher of a book decides whether an eBook can be loaned to others. If a publisher hasn't granted that right, the option to lend the book is not available.

You can determine whether a book can be loaned to others by reviewing the Product Details for the book on Amazon's website. If the book can be loaned, it displays "Lending: Enabled." Unfortunately, this information is not available from the Kindle Store listings on the Kindle Fire.

Subscribing to Periodicals

The Kindle Store offers a wide array of newspapers and magazines, including some that are optimized with multimedia content specifically for the Kindle Fire.

1. From the Home screen, tap Newsstand to open the Newsstand.

2. Tap Store to open the Kindle Newsstand.

3. Choose a magazine or newspaper you want to read.

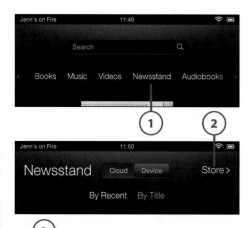

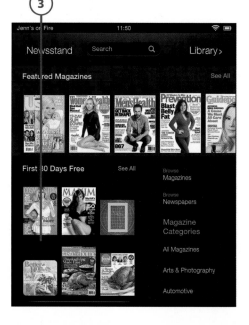

4. Tap Subscribe Now to download the latest edition to your Kindle Fire or Buy Issue to buy and download only the current issue.

Trial Subscriptions

Most periodicals provide a trial subscription, during which you are not charged. Unless you cancel your subscription within the trial period, you are charged the day after the trial concludes and monthly thereafter.

>>>Go Further

SIDELOADING BOOKS

Sources of eBooks abound, even beyond Amazon. After you download a Kindle-compatible eBook, you can transfer it to your Kindle using the micro-USB cable. Manually transferring files from your computer to your Kindle is called sideloading, and Chapter 2, "Loading Your Kindle Fire," covers it.

An easier way to sideload books, if you're using Windows or Linux, is to use Calibre. This application can organize your eBook library and even automatically convert eBooks in non-Kindle formats to a Kindle-compatible format. See Chapter 5, "Managing Content with Calibre," to learn more.

Organizing Your Books

The Kindle has always been a great device for reading. Instead of carrying around a pile of books, you can put everything you want to read on your Kindle. You can easily look up definitions with the integrated dictionary. You can search the Web when you want to read more about something you encounter in a book. You can even increase the size of a book's text to make it easier to read.

Browsing Your Library

After you buy or borrow a book or download a sample from the Kindle Store, it appears in the Books library and in the Carousel on the Home screen. You can view books on your device and in the cloud using the Books library.

1. From the Home screen, tap Books to access your Books library.

2. Tap Device to see content that has been downloaded to your Kindle Fire, or tap Cloud to see content that is in your online library.

3. Tap By Author, By Recent, or By Title to change the order in which your books are sorted.

Downloading a Book to Your Device

Before you can read a book, you must download it to your device.

1. From the Books library, tap Cloud to see the books in your online library.

2. Scroll to the book you want to download to your device.

3. Tap the book to download it to your device. You can also tap and hold the book and then tap Download.

Cloud and Device

When you are in Cloud view, you see books that are also on your device. That's because, even after you download a book to your device, it's still in the cloud so that you can download it to other Kindles or devices.

Books that you have downloaded to your device have a check mark in the lower-right corner.

Removing a Book from Your Device

You can remove downloaded books from your Kindle Fire to free up memory on the device. Your books will still be available in the cloud, so you can download them again at any time.

1. From the Books library, tap Device to see the books on your device.

2. Scroll to the book that you want to remove from your device.

3. Tap and hold the book.

4. Tap Remove from Device.

Reading on Your Kindle

The Kindle Fire is a great device for reading. Its backlit screen allows you to easily read in low-light conditions without a reading light. Your book always opens to the page you last read, so you don't have to worry about dog-earing pages or losing your place. If you don't know the meaning of a word, you can look up the definition on the spot.

My Book Doesn't Open on Page One

Kindle books open at the beginning of the book, but the beginning isn't necessarily page one. The publisher of an eBook can choose any page as the beginning of a book. eBooks frequently open at a point after the front matter—the cover, table of contents, foreword, and dedication. You can use the Go To button to access this material.

Reading a Book

Books appear in your Books library and on the Home screen Carousel. Reading a book on the Kindle Fire is as simple as tapping your finger.

1. From the Books library or the Carousel, tap a book to open it for reading.

2. Tap the right side of a page or swipe from right to left to move forward one page.

3. Tap the left side of a page or swipe from left to right to move back one page.

Where Are the Page Numbers?

Some eBooks use location numbers; others use traditional page numbers. Because text can be repaginated based on the text size you use, location numbers provide a better sense of where you are in the book.

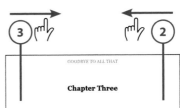

Navigating a Book

You can quickly access any page in a book, including the front matter.

1. Tap the center of the page.

2. Swipe the Location slider to move forward or backward within the book.

3. Tap the Go To button.

4. Tap the Go to Page or Location button to go to a specific location or page number.

5. Tap Sync to Furthest Page Read to return to the furthest page you've read in the book. If you have Whispersync turned on, as explained in Chapter 3, this button syncs to the furthest page you read on any of your Kindle devices or apps.

6. Tap Beginning to return to the first page of the book.

7. Tap Cover to see the book cover.

8. Tap Front Matter or a specific front matter element to see the table of contents, copyright page, and any other front matter the publisher chose to include.

9. Tap a chapter to go to the beginning of that chapter.

10. Tap the Back arrow to return to the page you were reading.

It's Not All Good

E Ink Versus LCD

Kindle devices have two types of displays: the E Ink on the Kindle e-readers and the LCD screen on the Kindle Fire. E Ink screens look very much like the printed page. They are very easy to read, and because they don't rely on a backlight, you can read an E Ink display in bright sunlight just as you can a printed page. The Kindle Paperwhite models shine light from above the E Ink, much like attaching a book light to your book or device, making it easy to read even in bed at night.

An LCD screen also has its own light source, but it's shined from the back of the display. Many people feel that reading an LCD screen is irritating to the eyes and can interfere with the body's circadian rhythm when viewed right before bed. However, because the Kindle Fire's screen is not as large as a computer monitor, it's generally less tiring to read on it.

Perhaps the biggest drawback to an LCD screen is that it can't be read comfortably in bright sunlight. Even the best LCD screens are washed out in bright daylight, and your Kindle Fire suffers from that same drawback. Don't expect to spend much time reading your Kindle Fire while relaxing on the beach. LCD screens also consume battery life faster, so if you take your Kindle Fire to the beach, plan to recharge by the end of the day.

Changing Font Styles

You can change the size of fonts, line spacing, page margins, and colors when reading Kindle content.

1. Tap the center of a page while you're reading.

2. Tap the Settings icon.

3. Tap the Font Size option to make the text larger or smaller. You can tap the appropriate button multiple times to get the size you want. The number between the larger and smaller buttons tells you the relative size of the font.

4. Tap a Color Mode to change the color of the page background and text.

5. Tap a Margins option to change the way the page is spread across the display.

6. Tap the Font option to select a different typeface.

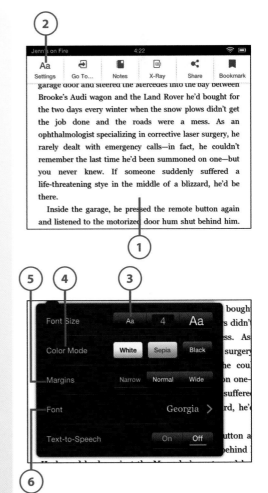

7. Choose a typeface from the options available.

Font Size and Typeface Are Not Just in Books

You can change font size and typeface settings in books, newspapers, personal documents, and magazines.

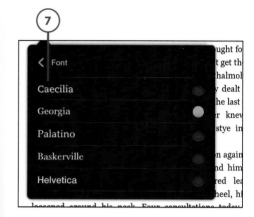

Looking Up Definitions

Your Kindle Fire comes with *The New Oxford American Dictionary* so that you can look up definitions of words while you're reading. Definitions are available from books, magazines, newspapers, and your personal documents.

1. Tap and hold the word you want to look up. A definition of the word displays.

2. Tap your book page to dismiss the pop-up definition.

3. Tap Full Definition to open the dictionary and see a more detailed definition.

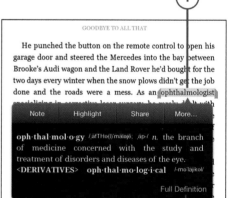

4. To return to your book after viewing a full definition, tap the center of the screen and then tap the Back icon.

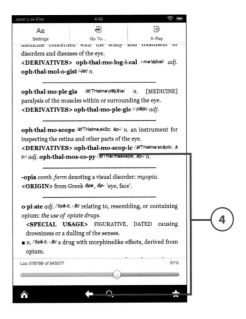

Working with Notes and Highlights

Just as when marking up a physical book, notes and highlights are a convenient way of annotating important passages. Notes are available in books and in personal documents that are in Mobi format. (Kindle files in Mobi format have either a .mobi or a .prc file extension.) Highlights are available in books and personal documents (that are in Mobi format), but you cannot highlight periodicals.

Notes enable you to visually locate a passage, along with personal comments that you attach to that passage. Highlights allow you to visually locate a passage again, but without personal comments.

Adding a Note

You can add a note to any book, whether you own the book or not. Notes that you add to a book are synchronized across all your Kindle devices and Kindle apps.

1. In an open book, tap and hold to begin selecting a passage to which you want to attach a note.

2. If necessary, tap and drag on the left and right of a selection to select more or fewer words.

3. Tap Note.

4. Enter the text for your note using the Kindle keyboard.

5. Tap Save to save the note.

6. To cancel a note, tap away from the Note pop-up.

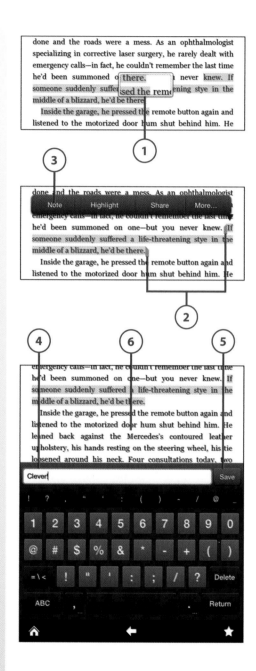

Viewing an Individual Note

Notes appear as highlighted text with a blue note icon. You can view an individual note by tapping it.

1. Tap the blue note icon that marks your note.

2. After reviewing your note, tap Close.

Editing a Note

You can easily edit notes, and any edits you make are synchronized across all your Kindle devices.

1. Tap the blue note icon that marks your note.

2. Tap Edit.

3. Enter the new text for your note.

4. Tap Save to commit your changes.

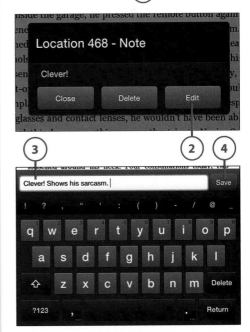

Deleting a Note

When you delete a note, you delete it across all your Kindle devices.

1. Tap the blue note icon that marks your note.

2. Tap Delete.

3. Tap Delete to confirm.

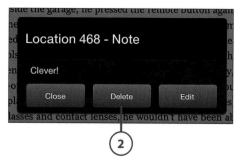

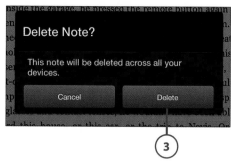

Adding a Highlight

As with the highlights in a physical book, a highlighted passage in a Kindle Fire book appears as yellow highlighted words.

1. Tap and hold to begin selecting a passage you want to highlight.

2. If necessary, tap and drag on the left and right of a selection to select more or fewer words.

3. Tap Highlight.

Viewing All Notes and Highlights

You can view a list of all your notes, highlights, and bookmarks for a particular book.

1. Tap the center of a page to access the Options bar.

2. Tap Notes to open the My Notes & Marks screen.

3. Scroll up and down to see all your notes and marks.

4. Tap a note or mark to go to that location in the book.

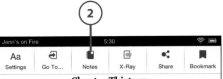

Deleting a Highlight

Unlike highlights in a physical book, you can delete a highlight in a Kindle book. The steps described here are also an alternative way to delete notes.

1. Tap the center of a page to access the Options bar.

2. Tap Notes to open the My Notes & Marks screen.

3. Locate the highlight (or note) you want to delete.

4. Tap and hold the highlight.

5. Tap Delete.

No Confirmation for Deleting Highlights

When you delete a highlight, you aren't asked whether you really want to delete it. If you think about it, this isn't a big deal because you can just highlight a passage again if you delete it in error.

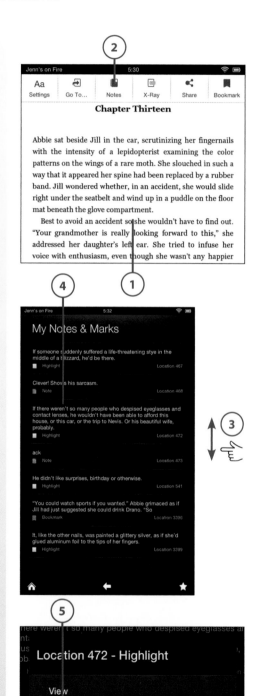

Working with Bookmarks

When you're reading a physical book, a bookmark enables you to mark your place so that you can easily return to it. The Kindle Fire marks your place automatically, but you still might want to add bookmarks on important pages so that you can easily locate them later. Think of these bookmarks as a dog-eared page. In fact, you can bookmark as many pages as you want in a book.

Bookmarks are available in books and in personal documents that are in Mobi format.

Adding a Bookmark

Adding a bookmark is easy. Bookmarks that you add are synchronized across all your Kindle devices and applications.

1. Move to the page where you want to add your bookmark.

2. Tap the middle of the page to bring up the Options bar.

3. Tap the Bookmark icon to add a bookmark.

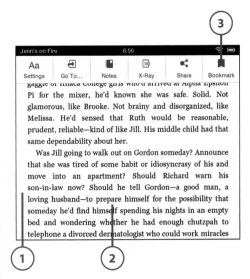

Removing a Bookmark

When you remove a bookmark, you remove it from all Kindle devices and applications.

1. Move to the page that is book-marked.

2. Tap the blue Bookmark icon to remove the bookmark.

Easy Bookmark Removal

Bookmarks can also be deleted from the My Notes and Marks screen. Tap and hold the bookmark you want to remove and tap Delete.

Moving to a Bookmark

You can easily move to a page that you've bookmarked using the My Notes & Marks screen.

1. Tap the center of a page while reading your book.

2. Tap the Notes icon.

3. Scroll to the bookmark.

4. Tap the bookmark to move directly to the bookmarked page.

Reading Magazines and Newspapers

The Kindle Fire is a wonderful way to read magazines and newspapers. The full-color screen and the touch interface make the experience of reading periodicals similar to that of reading a physical magazine.

Reading a Page View–Enabled Magazine

Many magazines that are available in the Kindle Store are Page View–enabled, which means that they provide two views: Page View and Text View. Page View represents the look of the actual printed magazine. Text View reformats the article into pages, to enable you to more easily focus on the text of the article.

1. From Newsstand, tap a magazine that is Page View–enabled to open it.

2. Tap the center of a page to display page thumbnails.

3. Tap a page thumbnail to move to that page. The current page is outlined in blue.

4. Swipe across the thumbnails to quickly move through the pages.

5. Tap the Contents icon to see a list of articles.

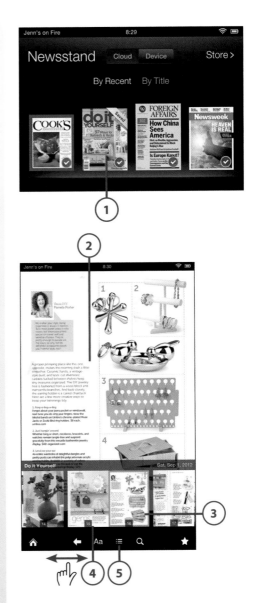

6. Tap an article to move directly to it.

7. Swipe left to move forward one page, or swipe right to move back one page. You can also tap the right edge of a page to page forward, and tap the left edge to page backward.

8. Reverse-pinch to zoom into a page.

9. Slide to move to a particular place on the page.

10. Pinch to zoom out.

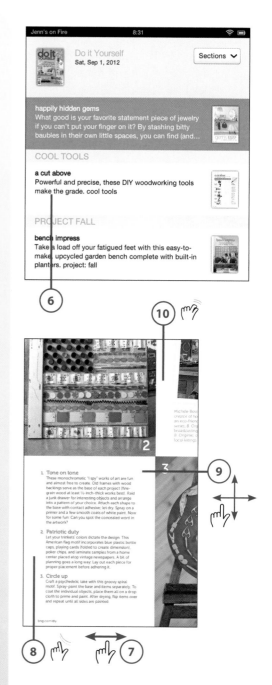

11. Double-tap a page to switch to Text View.

SALVAGE STYLE · FINDERS, KEEPERS

1. Tone on tone

These monochromatic "I spy" works of art are fun and almost free to create. Old frames with wood backings serve as the base of each project (fine-grain wood at least ½-inch-thick works best). Raid a junk drawer for interesting objects and arrange into a pattern of your choice. Attach each shape to the base with contact adhesive; let dry. Spray on a primer and a few smooth coats of white paint. Now for some fun: Can you spot the concealed word in the artwork?

2. Patriotic duty

Let your trinkets' colors dictate the design. This American flag motif incorporates blue plastic bottle caps, playing cards

Reading in Text View and Reading Newspapers

Magazines that aren't Page View–enabled always display in Text View and do not offer the option of displaying in Page View. The experiences of reading a magazine in Text View and reading a newspaper are identical.

1. From the Newsstand, tap a magazine that is not Page View–enabled or tap a newspaper.

2. Tap the center of a page to show the Progress and Options bars.

3. Tap the arrows on the Progress bar to move forward and backward through articles.

4. Tap the Text icon to change text size, typeface, and color options.

5. Tap the Contents icon to display a list of articles and sections.

6. Tap an article to go to that article.

7. Swipe left to move forward one page, or swipe right to move back one page. You can also tap the right or left edges of a page to move forward or backward.

Magazine and Newspaper Sections

Many magazines and newspapers have a Sections button in the upper right of the contents page to make it easy to navigate quickly to a specific section.

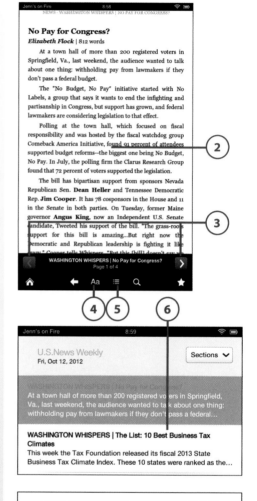

Listening to Audiobooks

Sometimes you want to read a good book, but perhaps you're driving or cooking and you don't have hands or eyes free to read it yourself. Audiobooks are audio editions of books, many of them read by celebrities or professional readers.

Not only can your Kindle Fire play audiobooks, but it can sync a bookmark across text and audio versions of the same book using Whispersync for Voice. You can also use Immersion Reading to follow along in the text while listening to the audiobook version.

Downloading Audiobooks

Audiobooks are sold in the Amazon Store through Audible. The first time you make an audiobook purchase, you're prompted to try a new Audible membership. If you already have an Audible account, you're asked to verify it.

1. Tap Audiobooks from the navigation bar.

2. Tap Store.

3. Select an audiobook.

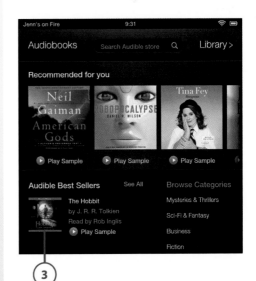

4. Play a sample if you want to hear the reader's voice before purchasing.

5. If this is your first Audible purchase, you receive an option to sign up for an Audible membership and download two free audiobooks.

6. If you already have an Audible membership, tap the Buy button to purchase the audiobook.

7. If you have an Audible account, but you've never purchased Audible audiobooks through the Amazon Store, verify your account. This links your Audible and Amazon accounts.

8. Tap Listen Now if you want to start listening to your audiobook immediately. If you have both the eBook and the audiobook of a title, this button says Read & Listen Now.

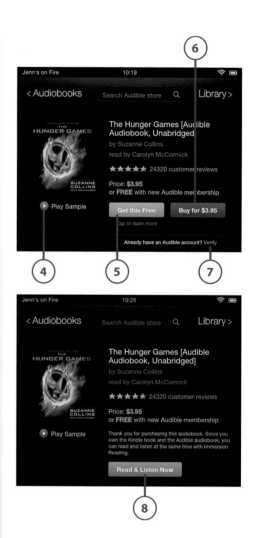

Listening to Audiobooks

Audiobooks are stored in the Amazon Cloud, available for download onto your device. Find your audiobooks in the Audiobooks library. Audiobooks are almost impossible to complete in one sitting, but don't worry about losing your place. Your Kindle Fire automatically syncs your audiobooks so you can start up again where you left off.

1. Tap Audiobooks in the navigation bar.

2. Tap an audiobook to play. If the audiobook has not yet been downloaded to your Kindle Fire, you must download it before you play it.

3. The audiobook automatically begins to play. Press Pause to temporarily stop the audio. Press Play to restart the audio.

4. Tap the Rewind 30 Seconds button to repeat the last 30 seconds of audio.

5. Tap Add Bookmark to add a bookmark to a point in the audio. Tap and hold to add a note.

6. Tap the Contents button to navigate to a specific chapter.

7. Swipe the location bar to play in a different location.

8. Choose the desired reading speed. Tap the turtle to decrease the reading speed, or tap the rabbit to increase it.

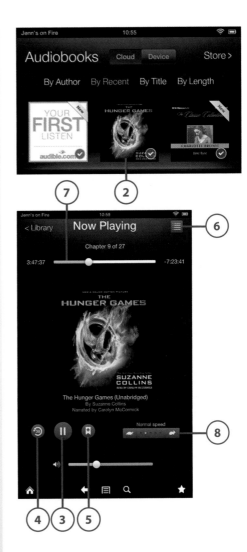

Viewing Bookmarks in Audiobooks

If you want to access bookmarks you set in an audiobook, tap the Menu icon in the Options bar and then tap View Bookmarks.

Setting a Sleep Timer

You can set a sleep timer to tell your Kindle Fire to automatically stop reading after a set amount of time.

1. Tap the Menu icon in the Options bar.

2. Tap Sleep Timer.

3. Set the amount of time you want the audiobook to play.

4. Tap End of Chapter if you want the audiobook to read to the end of the current chapter.

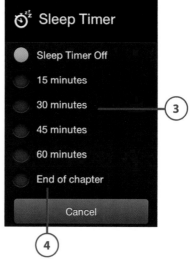

Immersion Reading

If you own both the eBook and audiobook versions of a book, you can use Immersion Reading to read along with the professional narrator.

1. Tap Books.

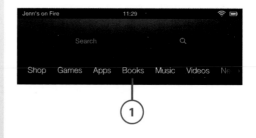

2. Tap the book you want to read and hear.

3. Tap the middle of the screen.

4. Tap Play to read with professional narration.

5. The gray highlights show the text the narrator is reading so you can follow along.

6. Tap Pause to pause the narration.

My Book Won't Sync

Immersion Reading is a new Kindle feature and is not without its flaws. Although it works well in most circumstances, it occasionally struggles to sync the eBook and audiobook, and you might have to tap the Play button several times to get it to work properly.

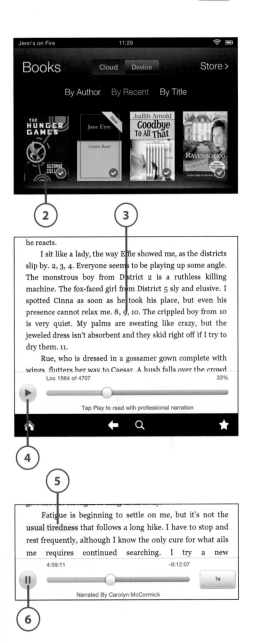

GETTING THE MOST OUT OF IMMERSION READING

Studies have shown that bimodal learning improves retention. If you're reading a book for academic purposes, such as Shakespeare, using Immersion Reading stimulates both your visual and your auditory senses, thereby helping you remember it later.

Using Text-to-Speech

Your Kindle Fire can read some books and periodicals even if you do not own the audiobook. Text-to-Speech reads in a very mechanical female voice, unlike the professional narration of audiobooks.

1. In a book, tap the middle of a page.

2. Tap Settings.

3. Tap the On button for Text-to-Speech.

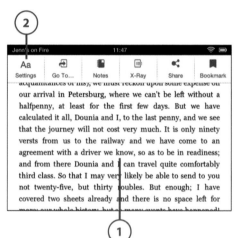

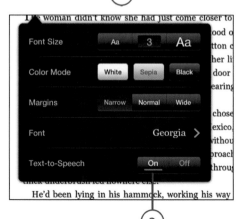

4. Tap the center of the page.

5. Tap Play to listen to Text-to-Speech. You can pause the narration with the same button.

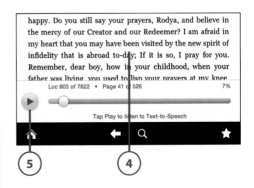

When Text-to-Speech Is Not Available

The publisher of a book determines whether the Text-to-Speech feature is available for that title.

Searching Content and Accessing Reference Materials

Your Kindle Fire provides several ways for you to get more information about your books. The device automatically maintains a searchable index of all the content in your libraries. You can also search in Wikipedia or Google. If you want to learn more about the book you're reading, X-Ray offers character breakdowns and other features.

Using X-Ray for Books

X-Ray shows you all the passages that refer to specific characters or terms. If you're reading a textbook, X-Ray can even act as a dynamic index.

1. Tap the middle of a page in the book you want to x-ray.

2. Tap X-Ray.

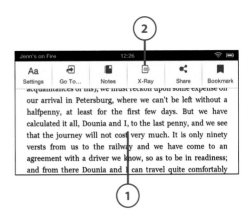

3. Examine the current page or chapter or the entire book.

4. Tap an entry to see a list of all references for that character or term.

5. Tap an entry to go to the source page for a reference.

Missing X-Rays

As with text-to-speech and certain other features, the availability of X-Ray is up to the publisher.

Searching the Current Item

You can search for one or more words in an item that you're reading.

1. While reading the item you want to search, tap the middle of a page.

2. Tap the Search icon.

3. Enter your search words in the Search box.

4. Tap Go.

5. Wait for the progress bar while the search completes.

6. Scroll to locate a specific search result.

7. Tap to move to the search result in the text.

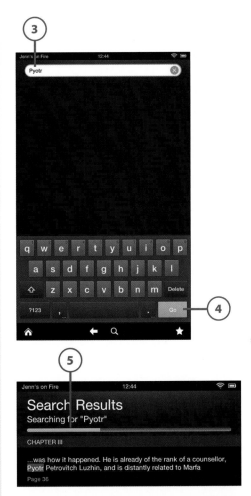

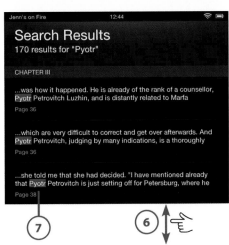

Searching Wikipedia or Google from Books

You can search the Web or Wikipedia for words that you select in books. If you select more than two words, these options aren't available.

1. Select one or two words you want to search for.

2. Tap More.

3. Tap Search Wikipedia to search for the selected word(s) in Wikipedia.

4. Tap Search the Web to search for the selected word(s) in your selected search engine.

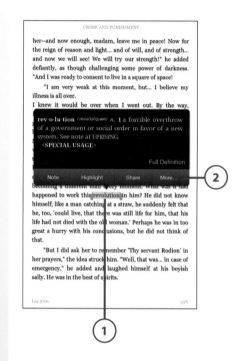

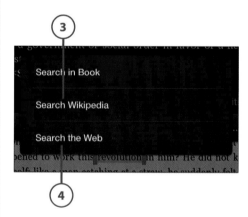

5. When you've finished reading the search results, tap the Back button to go back to your book.

Selecting a Search Engine

Your Kindle Fire uses Microsoft Bing as the default search engine. I explain how to change this in Chapter 12, "Browsing the Web with Silk."

Manage
eBooks on
your computer

Convert and
transfer to your
Kindle Fire

Edit author,
title, and
cover

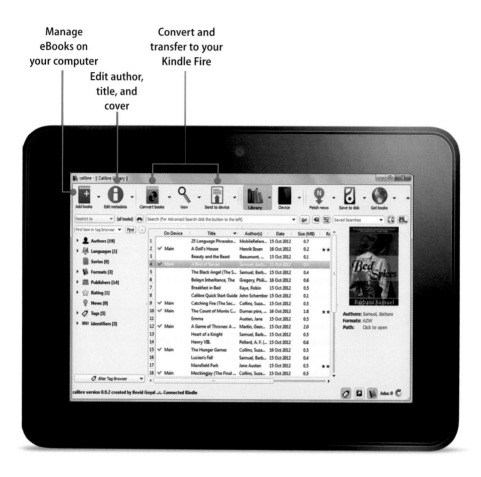

In this chapter, you learn how you can use a free tool called Calibre to manage eBooks that you download from sources other than Amazon.

→ Getting started with Calibre
→ Adding content to Calibre
→ Editing book information
→ Transferring eBooks to the Kindle Fire

5

Managing Content with Calibre

Amazon's Kindle Store offers millions of books that you can read on your Kindle Fire, but Amazon certainly doesn't have a corner on the eBook market. Sites such as www.feedbooks.com and www.fictionwise.com have plenty of eBooks that you can read on your Kindle.

Buying eBooks from Amazon gives you the benefit of having those eBooks stored in the cloud on Amazon's servers, an advantage that you don't get with third-party eBook vendors. However, by using a tool such as Calibre, you can easily manage your third-party eBooks.

Calibre Updates
Calibre is updated often, so by the time you read this chapter, the steps might have changed slightly. I wrote this chapter based on version 0.9.2 of Calibre.

Getting Started with Calibre

Calibre is a free eBook library management application for your computer. It organizes your eBook library, converts books into different formats, helps you locate books for purchase from dozens of eBook stores, and syncs your books onto all your eReader devices.

Calibre is available from www.calibre-ebook.com. Because you need to install Calibre on your computer, you must access the URL from your computer, not your Kindle Fire. Calibre is available for Windows, Mac OS X, and Linux. Go to the Download page on the Calibre website to access the version you need for your computer. Follow the download instructions for your operating system at the Calibre website.

It's Not All Good

Mac Users, Take Note

The Kindle Fire now uses Media Transfer Protocol (MTP) instead of USB Mass Storage. This might not sound like a big deal to most readers, but for Mac users, it's quite a blow. The Mac OS X does not recognize MTP, which means that transferring files to and from your Kindle Fire requires installation of a transfer app and extra steps that PC and Linux users do not have to undertake. Unfortunately, this also means that Mac users cannot use Calibre to side-load eBooks onto their Kindle Fire.

If you are a Mac user who already relies upon Calibre to maintain your eBook collection for an older Kindle device (including the first-generation Kindle Fire) or other eReader, this will undoubtedly cause frustration. You can e-mail your eBooks to the Kindle Fire, as explained at the end of this chapter, but your books will show up in the Docs library instead of your Books library. Another option is to run Calibre under Windows using Boot Camp, Parallels, or VMware Fusion, if you have one of those available. Taking this step, however, is outside the realm of this book.

Using the Welcome Wizard

After you've downloaded and installed Calibre, you can launch it and walk through the Welcome Wizard.

1. Choose your language.

2. Choose a folder for your Calibre library. If you've already downloaded eBooks to your computer that you want Calibre to manage, choose the folder that contains them. Otherwise, you can accept the default to create a new folder.

3. Click Next.

4. Select Amazon as the manufacturer and Kindle Fire as the device. (As you can see here, Calibre works with a host of eReader devices.)

5. Click Next.

6. Click Finish to start using Calibre.

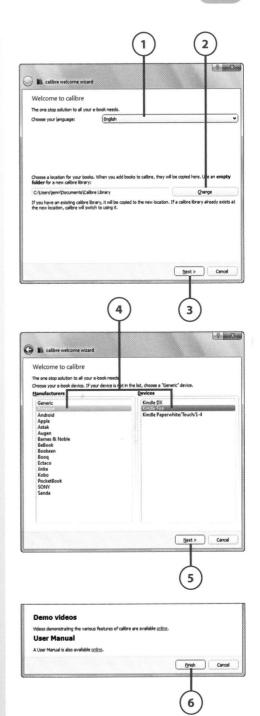

Adding Content to Calibre

If you already have eBooks in the folder you chose in the Welcome Wizard, Calibre should already be populated with your eBooks. Otherwise, you need to import any existing eBooks into Calibre.

Importing Books

You can import eBooks in any format into your Calibre library. If an eBook is in a format that your Kindle Fire doesn't recognize, Calibre can usually convert it for you.

1. Click Add Books.

2. Navigate to the folder on your computer that contains your eBooks.

3. Select one or more eBooks to add to your Calibre library.

4. Click the Open button to import the selected books into your library.

5. Wait until Calibre finishes importing your eBooks.

6. If Calibre notifies you that it found duplicates, click No so that they aren't imported.

Adding New Books

If you download new eBooks after you've built your Calibre library, you need to add them to Calibre using the Add Books button.

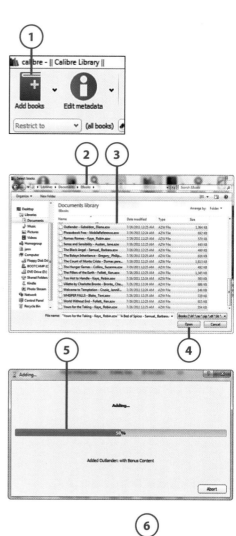

EBOOK FORMATS

eBooks come in many different formats. The most popular eBook format is called EPUB, and it's the format that libraries have used for the past several years. The Kindle is the only common eBook reader that does not support the EPUB format. Instead, the Kindle supports the MOBI format. eBooks that you purchase from the Kindle Store have an AZW extension, which is a form of MOBI that Amazon has modified to add its own digital rights management (DRM) so that you can't buy a book once and give it to a million Internet users. Other book formats might use a different form of DRM to protect against piracy.

Fortunately, converting books from EPUB and other formats into MOBI format is easy as long as the books are not protected with DRM, as I explain in this chapter. Unfortunately, if a book is protected with DRM, you need the correct type of eReader to view that book because it cannot legally be converted. Calibre warns you if you try to add a book to your Kindle Fire in an improper format.

Searching for New eBooks

Calibre has an integrated search engine that makes locating new eBooks easy. Calibre's search engine searches eBook stores on the Internet for the search term you enter, and many of these eBook stores sell books that are compatible with your Kindle Fire.

Calibre searches for either authors or titles. In other words, you can't enter "fantasy" to find fantasy books. Instead, you'll find books with "fantasy" in the title or books written by Mr. or Mrs. Fantasy.

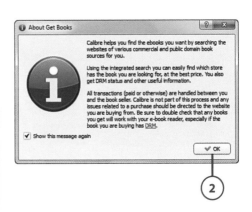

1. Click Get Books.

2. Click OK in the information dialog box.

3. Select the stores you want to search.

4. Enter your search query. Calibre searches using only the title and author.

5. Click Search.

6. Double-click a search result to view details in your web browser or to purchase the eBook. Online bookstores use various means to connect you to your purchases, so follow the site's instructions to complete your transaction and obtain your books.

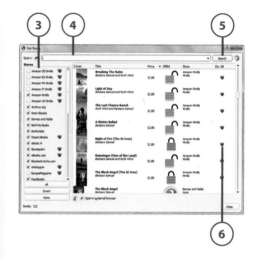

Pay Attention to DRM

Pay special attention to the DRM status of eBooks. If you see a red lock next to a search result, it means that the eBook is protected with DRM and can be read only on certain devices. Your Kindle Fire supports only Amazon Kindle DRM. If a book is DRM protected and it isn't from the Amazon Kindle Store, it won't open on your Kindle. Books with a green lock are not protected with DRM and can generally be converted to a format that will open on your Kindle. Books in Kindle AZW format also appear with a green lock because they can be viewed on your Kindle Fire, which you set as your device in the Welcome Wizard.

It's Not All Good

Use Caution When Searching

Some eBooks that you can find online might be copyrighted books that are being offered illegally. It's not a bad idea to search for eBooks only from sources that you know are legitimate. For example, if a site is offering an eBook for free and that same eBook costs $10 everywhere else, that's a good sign that something's not right. Downloading pirated books is a copyright infringement and keeps the author from being compensated for the work. It also leads to publishers putting further DRM restrictions on eBooks, which can limit your ability to lend books or access them in other formats.

Editing Book Information

Some of your eBooks might not display the correct author or title. The most common cause of this for Kindle users relates to personal docs e-mailed to your Kindle e-mail address. When Amazon converts these documents, it uses the sending e-mail for the author name. It's easy to use Calibre to edit the author, title, and other information about an eBook.

Downloading Metadata

Calibre can locate information about a particular eBook using well-known book sources such as Amazon and Google.

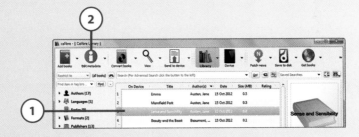

1. Select the book you want to edit.

2. Click Edit Metadata.

3. Click Download Metadata.

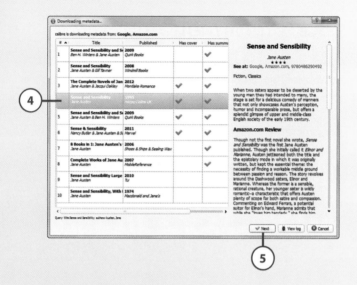

4. Click the title that matches your search.

5. Click Next.

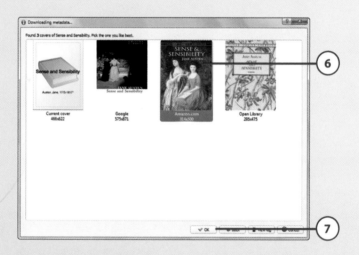

6. Click a cover picture for your book. Not all results include a book cover.

7. Click OK.

(8)

8. Click OK to add the new metadata to your eBook.

Better Metadata Searching

If you don't find a result when downloading metadata, try adding an ISBN number (you can get it by searching the Books section at Amazon) to the IDs text box and then clicking Download Metadata.

>>>Go Further

FINDING COVERS

Some eBooks, particularly those in the public domain, are not embedded with the same cover art that the print copies use. Calibre can usually locate a cover for your eBooks, but if it can't, an Internet search usually turns up a cover. When you locate one, save the image to your computer, edit the metadata for the book in Calibre, and use the Change Cover tools to browse to the image and attach it to your eBook.

Manually Editing Metadata

If Calibre can't find your eBook when you try to download metadata, you can edit the metadata manually. You can also enter additional metadata for a book. The more metadata is in a record, the easier it is to catalogue it and search for the book later.

1. Open the Metadata dialog box as described in the previous section.

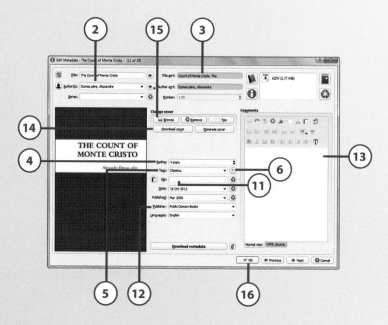

2. Correct the title or author's name, if necessary.

3. Correct the way the title or author's name appears when sorting by title or author. In the example, you can change the Author sort to "Dumas père, Alexandre" so that it appears in proper order by last name.

4. If you've already read the book, give it a rating.

5. Tag the book by genre or theme.

6. Open the Tag Editor to edit the list of tags.

7. Type the new tag. It can be a genre, a theme, or any other keyword you want.

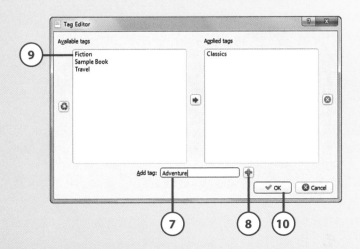

8. Click the plus sign to add the new tag.

9. Double-click an available tag to apply other tags to the book.

10. Click OK.

11. Add the ISBN for the book.

12. Change the publication and language information if it is incomplete or incorrect.

13. You can add your own comments or a review of the book. Use the formatting options to format your comments.

14. If you need to add a cover, click Download Cover.

15. If Calibre cannot locate a cover, but you downloaded one from another source, click Browse to locate the downloaded file, then navigate to the file and click OK.

16. Click OK to save your changes.

Transferring eBooks to the Kindle Fire

To use Calibre to sideload books onto your Kindle Fire, you first convert the eBook to a proper format, if necessary, and then transfer the file. The best format for transferring books onto your Kindle Fire is MOBI. If you follow the steps in the next section, your sideloaded books appear in the Books library along with your Kindle Store book purchases.

What About E-mailing Books?

If you e-mail books to your Kindle, they are stored in the Docs library, which means they're separated from your other books. This process is often less time consuming because you can usually provide your Kindle e-mail address to the online bookstore and have your purchases automatically e-mailed to your device. However, if you want to keep all your books together, sideloading through Calibre is the way to go. Instead of having books e-mailed directly to your Kindle, download your purchases onto your computer, add them to your Calibre library, and proceed from there.

Converting to MOBI Format

If your book is already in MOBI or EPUB format, this step is unnecessary. If your book is in any other format, however, you should convert the eBook to MOBI format before transferring it to your Kindle Fire.

Kindle Fire and EPUB Format

The Kindle Fire cannot read EPUB format, but Calibre can automatically convert books from EPUB to MOBI while uploading to the Kindle Fire. This conversion process still allows your books to show up correctly in your Books library.

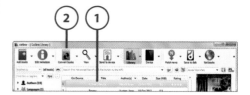

1. Select the book you want to convert.

2. Click Convert Books.

3. Change the Output Format to MOBI.

4. Check Use Cover from Source File.

5. Click MOBI Output.

6. Change the Personal Doc Tag to [EBOK].

7. Click OK. A jobs icon in the lower-right corner spins as Calibre processes the conversion.

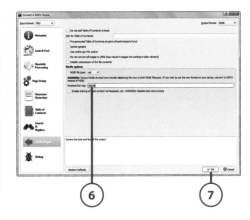

⑥   ⑦

Deleting Non-MOBI Formats

If you intend to make the Kindle Fire your only eReader device, you need to keep only the MOBI format in your Calibre library. Save space by deleting unused formats.

①

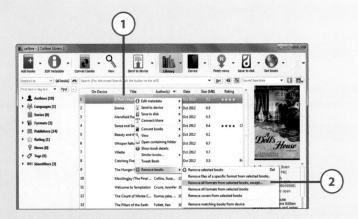

②

1. Right-click the book you just converted.

2. Point to Remove Books and click Remove All Formats from Selected Books, Except.

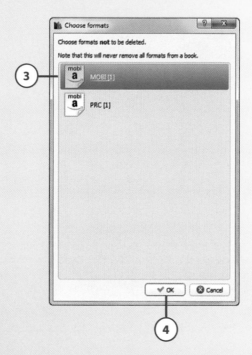

3. Select the MOBI format. This is the format you want to keep.
4. Click OK.

Transferring an eBook to Your Kindle

Now that you have a MOBI copy of your eBook in your Calibre library, you can transfer the eBook to your Kindle Fire. Before you complete these steps, make sure your Kindle Fire is connected to your computer with the mini-USB cable.

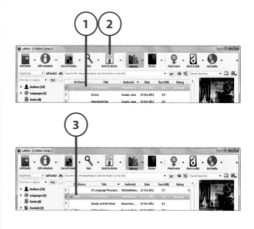

1. Select the eBook you want to transfer.

2. Click Send to Device.

3. Wait until Calibre shows that the eBook is on your device.

Transferring an EPUB Format eBook

If you choose to use EPUB-format eBooks, Calibre can automatically convert the EPUB format to one that is compatible with your Kindle Fire. After completing step 2, click Yes when asked whether you want to convert the eBook.

Finding the Sideloaded Book

You can find the book that you sideloaded to your Kindle Fire in your Books library. It also appears on the Carousel on the Home screen.

E-mailing eBooks to Your Kindle

Calibre can e-mail eBooks to your Kindle account. The eBook must already be in Microsoft Word (.doc or .docx), Rich Text, HTML, text, or MOBI format. Remember, e-mailed books show up in the Docs library, not the Books library, on your Kindle Fire.

Good News for Mac Users

This feature works for Mac users as well as PC and Linux users. At this time, this is the only way for Mac users to transfer books from Calibre to the Kindle Fire.

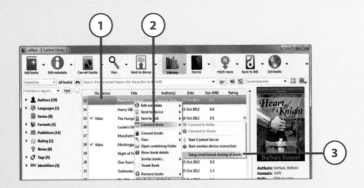

1. Right-click the book that you want to e-mail to your Kindle e-mail address.

2. Point to Connect/Share.

3. Select Setup E-mail Based Sharing of Books.

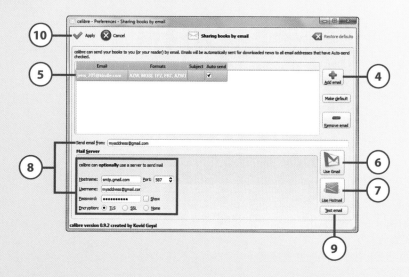

4. Click Add E-mail.

5. Enter your Kindle e-mail address. (Tap Docs on your Kindle Fire to find your Kindle e-mail address if you're not sure.)

6. Click Use Gmail and enter your Gmail information if you want to use a Gmail account to send the e-mail. This option automatically fills in the server information to send messages and eBooks through Gmail's servers.

7. Click Use Hotmail and enter your Hotmail information if you want to use a Hotmail account to send the e-mail. This option automatically fills in the server information.

8. If you don't want to use Hotmail or Gmail, enter your e-mail address and server information. If you don't know your e-mail server information, check with your Internet Service Provider.

9. Click Test E-mail to test your e-mail settings.

10. Click Apply.

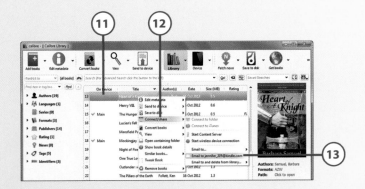

11. Again, right-click the book you want to send.

12. Point to Connect/Share.

13. Select E-mail for the address you set up in steps 6–8.

Use an Approved E-mail

The e-mail address that you configure in Calibre needs to be an e-mail that is on your approved e-mail list for sending docs to your Kindle Fire. For details on adding an e-mail to the approved e-mail list, see "Adding an Approved E-mail for Docs" in Chapter 3, "Using Amazon's Manage Your Kindle Page."

EXTENDING YOUR CALIBRE KNOW-HOW

>>>Go Further

If you enjoy organizing your books in Calibre, you can get more out of this versatile app. In Calibre Preferences, you can get plug-ins to add new features. Look for the Goodreads Sync plug-in to link your library to your Goodreads account, Count Pages to estimate how many pages are in EPUB and MOBI files, and Reading List to organize your list of books to be read.

View Your Cloud
and Device Music

Use
Playlists

Browse
Music

Play
Music

Jenn's on Fire   2:39

Music   Cloud   **Device**   Store >

Playlists   Artists   Albums   Songs

All Their Greatest ...
Barenaked Ladies

Babel
Mumford & Sons

The Battle For Ev...
Five For Fighting

The Best Of 1980...
U2

The Best Of Tho...
Various Artists

Born On A Pirate ...
Barenaked Ladies

Brand New Day
Sting

Brand New Eyes
Paramore

Brothers In Arms
Dire Straits

Buckshot LeFonq...
Buckshot LeFonque

Buscando
Quetzal Guerrero

The Clapton Chro...
Eric Clapton

Oblivion
Lucia Micarelli - Music From A Farther Room

In this chapter, you learn how to access and listen to music on your Kindle Fire. Topics include the following:

→ Browsing and downloading your music
→ Searching for music
→ Playing music
→ Managing playlists
→ Buying new music

6

Accessing and Listening to Music

The Kindle Fire is arguably the best way to play music that you have stored on Amazon's Cloud Player. Because it has a limited amount of user-accessible memory, you likely can't carry all your music on it when you're offline, but you can make playlists and download some of your music to enjoy when you're away from a Wi-Fi connection.

In addition to playing music, you can browse Amazon's extensive library of MP3s to add to your music collection.

Browsing and Downloading Your Music

Your Kindle Fire integrates directly into your Cloud Drive and provides a first-class interface into browsing and listening to your music. As soon as you start your Kindle Fire for the first time (after you've signed into your Amazon account on the device), it begins indexing the music on your Cloud Drive.

This chapter deals primarily with music in the cloud because that's likely the way you'll listen to music on your Kindle Fire. However, all the information presented also applies to interacting with music stored on your device.

Add Music to Your Cloud Drive

If you haven't added any music to your Cloud Drive, see Chapter 2, "Loading Your Kindle Fire," for information on how to do that.

Browsing Artists

Your Kindle Fire can provide you with a list of all artists in your music collection, in alphabetical order.

1. From the Home screen, tap Music.

2. Tap Cloud to view your Cloud Drive.

3. Tap Artists to display artists in your collection.

4. Scroll up and down to view artists.

5. Tap an artist to see a list of albums in your collection by the artist.

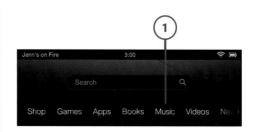

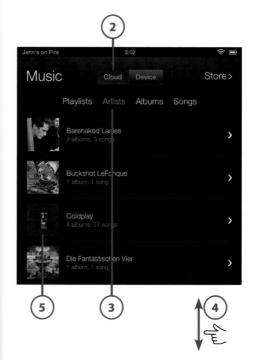

6. Tap Songs to see a list of all songs by the artist.

7. Tap Shop This Artist to open the Amazon MP3 Music Store, where you can buy songs and albums by the artist you are viewing.

8. Tap Download All to download all the songs by the artist you have stored in your Cloud Drive to your device.

9. Tap an album to see details on the album.

10. Tap Download All to download the album to your device.

11. Tap Music to quickly go back to a list of artists to choose a new artist.

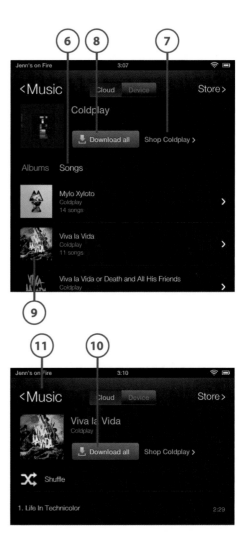

Browsing Albums and Songs

You can use the same technique to browse albums and songs on your Cloud Drive.

When you are viewing a list of albums from an artist, you can tap and hold an album and then tap Download Album to download it.

Scrolling Quickly in Music

Having a large number of artists, albums, or songs in your music collection is not uncommon. To more quickly find an item, you can scroll to items that begin with a particular letter of the alphabet.

This technique works in all lists in your Music library.

1. From a list of music items, tap and drag to begin scrolling.

2. As soon as the scroll handle appears, immediately tap and hold it.

3. Drag the scroll handle up and down to quickly browse by letter.

4. Release the scroll handle when the desired letter appears on the screen to jump to items that begin with that letter.

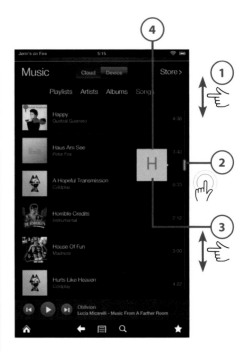

Monitoring Downloads from an Album

As your music tracks are being downloaded, you can monitor their progress and cancel the download, if necessary.

1. Locate an artist, album, or song you want to download.

2. Tap Download All.

3. Tap the X if you want to cancel the download for a particular song.

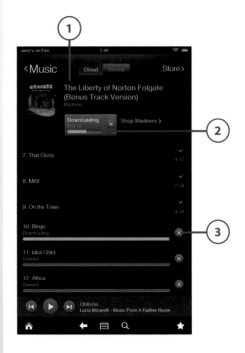

4. Tap Cancel Download.

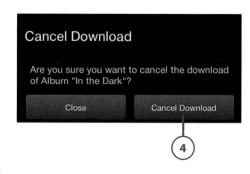

Monitoring All Music Downloads

If you're downloading music from several albums or artists, you can monitor the progress of all the downloads at once.

1. From any screen in your Music library, tap the Menu icon.

2. Tap Downloads.

3. Tap the Pause/Resume icon to pause or resume the current download.

4. Tap See Completed Downloads to see a list of tracks that have already been downloaded.

Latest Additions Playlist

When you view completed downloads, you're actually looking at an automatic playlist called Latest Additions. This playlist is also available on the Playlists screen.

Canceling Downloads

You can cancel pending downloads. Any tracks that have already downloaded remain on your device.

1. While viewing active downloads, tap and hold the item that's currently downloading.

2. Tap Cancel Download.

It's Not All Good

Seeing the Music on Your Device

Occasionally when you download music from the cloud to your device, you won't see it in the Device list. If you look at the song or album in the Cloud list, it appears to be downloaded (as evidenced by the check mark in the right corner), and you can play it immediately, but it simply doesn't appear in the Device list. The only way I've found to correct this problem is to power down the Kindle Fire and start it up again. Your music then shows up properly in the Device list.

Searching for Music

Sometimes you have a burning desire to listen to a particular song. Of course, you can scroll through your song list on the Kindle Fire to find it, but if you have thousands of songs, it's often easier to search for what you want to hear.

Searching Your Music Collection

Your Kindle Fire can search both music that's on your device and music in the cloud. You can search for playlists, artists, albums, or songs.

1. In the Music app, tap the Search icon.

2. Enter your search term in the Search box. Results appear as you type.

3. Tap the item you seek. The search results list items from both the cloud and the device.

Sorting Through Search Results

If you are in the Music app when you begin your search, the first set of search results is from your Music library. These results are followed by a count of items matching your search term from other Kindle Fire apps.

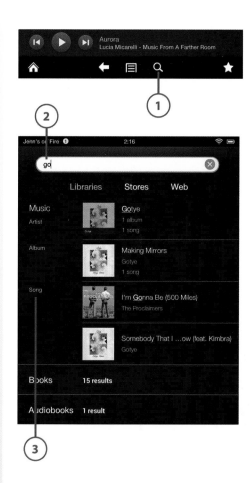

Playing Music

Your Kindle Fire can play music you've downloaded to the device or stream music directly from your Cloud Drive. When you stream music, you need a Wi-Fi (or 4G) connection. If you're going to be in an area where you cannot connect to the Internet, plan ahead by downloading music so that it will be available no matter where you go.

Listening to Music

You can play music either through the speakers built into the Kindle Fire or through headphones or an external speaker system. After you begin playing music, you can do other tasks on your Kindle Fire, such as read a book or send an e-mail, while the music continues playing.

1. Locate and tap the song you want to hear. This brings up the Now Playing screen.

2. Tap or drag the location slider to move to a particular point in the song. As you drag it, an indicator displays your position in the song.

3. Tap Previous to move to the previous song.

4. Tap Next to move to the next song.

5. Tap or drag the Volume slider to adjust the volume of playback.

6. Tap the left side of the Volume slider to instantly mute the audio.

7. Tap the right side of the Volume slider to instantly change to full volume.

8. Tap Shuffle to randomly play the songs in the Now Playing queue. Tap it again to turn off shuffle playback.

9. Tap Repeat to repeat all the songs in the Now Playing queue. Tap Repeat again to repeat only the currently playing song.

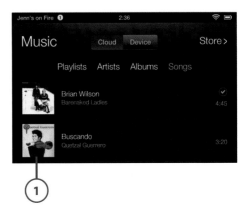

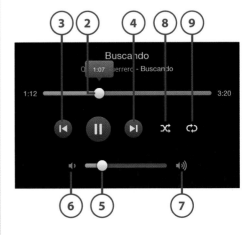

Accessing More Options

While viewing the Now Playing screen, tap and hold the album art for a menu of other ways you can interact with your music, including adding the song to a playlist, shopping for more music by the artist, and downloading the song (if you're currently streaming it) to your device.

Accessing Music Controls

You don't have to remain in the Music app while playing music. You can access playback controls or see the title and artist of the song that's currently playing while in any other app.

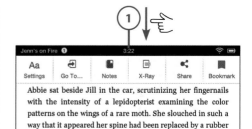

1. Swipe down from the status bar. If you're reading a book or periodical, tap the middle of the page first to display the status bar.

2. Tap the Pause button to pause the music.

3. Tap the Previous button to move to the previous song.

4. Tap the Next button to move to the next song.

5. Tap the name of the song to bring up the Now Playing screen.

6. Swipe up from the bottom of the screen to return to what you were doing.

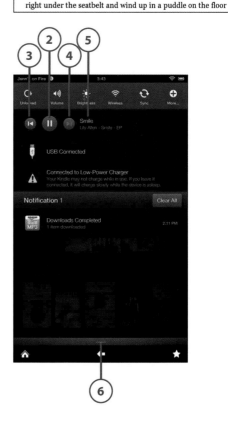

Managing Playlists

Playlists enable you to create a list of tracks that you want to play. You can create playlists on your device or in the cloud. If you create a playlist in the cloud, that playlist can be accessed both from your computer and from another device that can access your Cloud Player.

Creating a Playlist

You create playlists on your device by first tapping the Device tab. If you tap the Cloud tab first, your playlist is created on your Cloud Player. Playlists that you create on your device can contain only songs that are downloaded to your device. Playlists that you create on your Cloud Player can contain any of your music that is on your Cloud Player.

1. From your Music library, tap Playlists.

2. Tap Cloud to create a playlist from tracks in your Cloud Player, or tap Device to create a playlist from tracks on your device.

3. Tap Create New Playlist.

4. Enter a name for your playlist.

5. Tap Save.

6. Add songs to your playlist by tapping the + sign next to the song.

7. Tap the Search Your Device Music field and enter a song, album, or artist name to search for tracks.

8. Tap Done when finished adding songs.

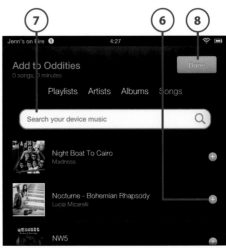

Cannot Move Device Playlist to the Cloud

When you create a playlist on your device, that playlist can contain only songs that are on your device. You cannot move a playlist created on your device to the cloud.

Editing a Playlist

After you've created a playlist and added your initial songs, you can add or remove songs by editing the playlist.

1. From the Playlists screen, tap your playlist.

2. Tap Edit.

3. Tap the minus sign to remove a song from the playlist.

4. Tap and hold the dots at the left edge of a song, and drag to a new position in the playlist to reorder songs.

5. Tap the Add Songs button to add new songs using the same interface you used when creating the playlist.

6. Tap Done to save your changes.

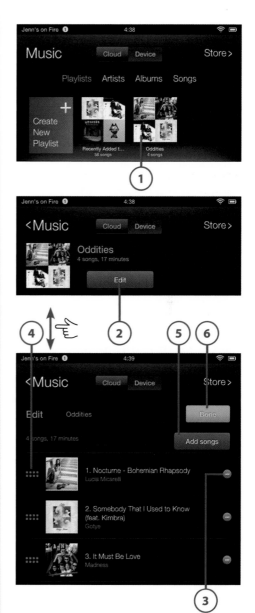

Adding Artists or Albums to a Playlist

You can add songs to a playlist when you edit the playlist, as I just explained, or whenever you come across music you want to add. Instead of adding songs one track at a time, you can also add all songs by an artist or in a particular album.

1. Tap and hold the song, artist, or album that you want to add to a playlist.

2. Tap Add to Playlist.

3. If you want to add the music to the most recent playlist, tap Add to (the name of the playlist).

4. Tap the playlist to which you want to add the music. Alternatively, tap Create New Playlist to create a new playlist.

5. If creating a new playlist, give it a name.

6. Tap Save to save the new playlist.

Playing a Playlist

Playlists that are on your device can be played only on your Kindle Fire. When you create playlists in the cloud, you can play them on your Kindle Fire or other devices that can access your Cloud Player.

1. From your Music library, tap Playlists.

2. Tap Cloud to see playlists on your Cloud Drive, or tap Device to see playlists on your Kindle Fire.

3. Tap the playlist you want to play.

4. Tap a song in the playlist to start playing from that song onward.

5. Tap Shuffle to play the songs in random order.

Downloading a Playlist

You can't play playlists that you create in your Cloud Drive unless you have an active Internet connection. If you want to play the playlist when you aren't connected, you first need to download the playlist to your device.

1. From the Playlists screen, tap Cloud.

2. Tap the playlist that you want to download.

3. Tap the Download All button to download the playlist to your device.

Downloaded Playlist

Downloaded playlists appear on the Device tab in the Playlists screen. Both the playlist and all songs in the playlist are downloaded.

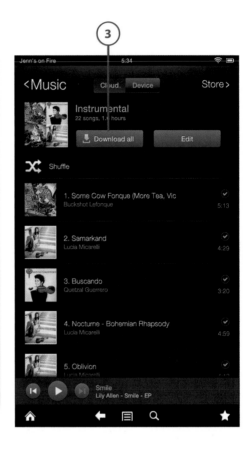

It's Not All Good

The Same Playlist, but Different

When you download a playlist from the cloud to your device, it is initially an identical match. In essence, however, you have created two different playlists. If you edit one playlist, your changes are not reflected in the other playlist. I recommend changing the name of one of the playlists after downloading it so you don't confuse them.

I also recommend creating and editing all your playlists in the cloud, even if you choose to also download them to your device. If you edit a playlist in the cloud, you can always download the updated playlist to your device again, whereas you can't upload a playlist you created or modified on your Fire back up to the cloud.

Renaming a Playlist

If you decide to change the name of a playlist, you can rename it from the Playlists screen.

1. From the Playlists screen, tap the playlist you want to rename.

2. Tap Edit.

3. Tap the current name of the playlist and enter a new name for the playlist.

4. Tap Done.

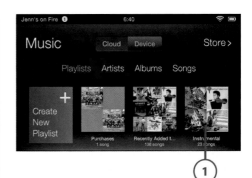

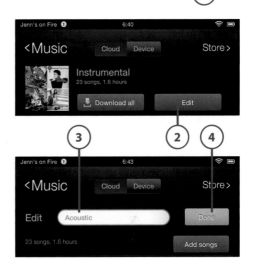

Deleting a Playlist

When you no longer want to keep a playlist, you can delete it. Deleting a playlist doesn't affect the songs themselves; it only removes the playlist.

When you delete a cloud playlist, it becomes inaccessible to all devices that access your Cloud Player.

1. From the Playlists screen, tap and hold the playlist you want to delete.

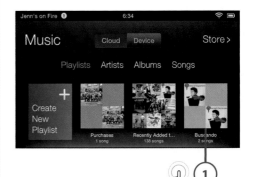

2. If you're deleting a cloud playlist, Tap Delete Playlist from Cloud. If you're deleting a device playlist, tap Remove Playlist from Device.

3. Tap Yes to confirm the deletion.

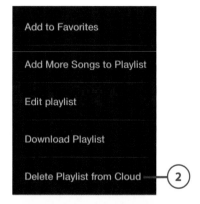

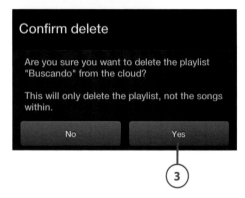

Buying New Music

You can purchase new music from Amazon's MP3 Music Store on your Kindle Fire. You can choose whether music that you purchase is added only to your Cloud Player or added to your Cloud Player and then automatically downloaded to your device.

Navigating the Music Store

The Music Store is accessible from your Music library.

1. From any screen in your Music library, tap Store to go to the Music Store.

2. Scroll through featured songs and albums.

3. Tap a category to see more music.

4. Tap See All to see more music of that type, such as the New Releases category, to see all new album releases.

5. Scroll through Recommended for You to see recommended music.

6. Tap Search to search for music.

7. Tap any item to see details, listen to sample tracks, and purchase music.

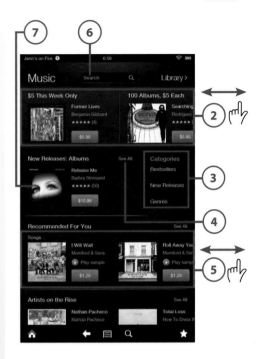

Sampling and Buying Music

As you're browsing the Music Store, you can sample 30 seconds of songs or purchase songs.

1. Tap a song or album.

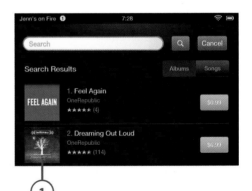

2. Tap the Play Sample button to listen to a 30-second sample of a song.

3. Tap the song price to purchase the song.

4. Tap the album price to purchase the entire album.

5. Tap Shop Artist to see all music by that artist.

Sampling Multiple Songs

When a 30-second sample finishes for one song, your Kindle Fire automatically starts playing a 30-second sample of the next song in the album.

>>>Go Further

ALBUM ONLY

Some songs are listed as Album Only and cannot be purchased individually. This restriction most often appears on extra content, such as digital booklets, that accompany some albums. It might also appear on compilation albums in which particular songs are sold as part of the compilation and not individually. If you want to access this content, you must purchase the complete album.

Changing Music Delivery Preferences

When you purchase music, it is added to your Cloud Player. You can also choose to have your music automatically downloaded to your device.

1. Swipe down from the status bar to open Settings.

2. Tap More.

3. Tap Applications.

4. Scroll down and tap Music.

5. Tap the On button to automatically download music purchases to your device, or tap Off to store your music only on your Cloud Player.

Buy Now, Download Later

Of course, don't forget that you can always download music from your Cloud Player to your device at any time. Turning this setting to Off gives you more control over exactly which music is stored on your device at any given time.

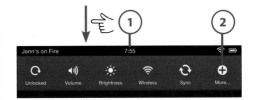

ACQUIRING MUSIC FROM OTHER SOURCES

>>>Go Further

Many other sources for digital music exist, including the iTunes Store and eMusic.com. Music must be in non-DRM AAC, MP3, MIDI, OGG, or WAV format to be accessible on the Kindle Fire. Use the Amazon Cloud Player website to add music to your Cloud Player, or sideload music from Windows Explorer (on the PC) or using the Android File Transfer app (on the Mac). You find instructions for using the Cloud Player and sideloading in Chapter 2.

Stream instantly
over Wi-Fi

Watch your
favorite movies
and TV shows

Watch Amazon Prime
videos for free

Create a Watchlist
for later viewing

In this chapter, you learn how to take advantage of the video capabilities of your Kindle Fire and explore how you can use your device to watch your own videos. Topics include the following:

→ Navigating the Video Store
→ Working with your video library
→ Sideloading videos

Watching Video on Your Kindle Fire

Your Kindle Fire is an excellent device for watching videos. The Kindle Fire HD provides high-definition (720p) video and Dolby Digital sound for a great theatrical experience that you can hold in your hands. Amazon offers more than 100,000 movies and TV shows that you can watch immediately on your Kindle Fire, and if you're a Prime member, you can find thousands of movies and TV shows that you can watch at no extra charge.

Navigating the Video Store

You can rent or purchase movies and TV shows from the Video Store. Amazon automatically synchronizes your playback location so you can start watching on one device and finish on another.

If you're an Amazon Prime member, you can instantly watch many movies or TV shows as part of your annual membership fee. These videos are streamed, so you can watch them only if you have a Wi-Fi (or 4G) connection.

You can also rent or purchase videos, which gives you the option of streaming or downloading the video to your Kindle Fire for offline viewing at your convenience. Keep in mind that even if a video is offered for free streaming with Amazon Prime, you still pay the rental or purchase fee if you prefer to download it to your device.

Video Store or Library

When you are connected to Wi-Fi (or 4G), tapping Videos on the home screen launches the Video Store. However, if you aren't connected to Wi-Fi, tapping Videos takes you to your video library.

Browsing the Video Store

Access the Video Store from your home screen.

1. Tap Videos to access the Video Store.

2. Tap in the Search box to search for videos.

3. Scroll to view recommended titles.

4. Tap See More to view all Prime Instant Videos.

5. Tap Movies or TV or see videos of that type.

6. Scroll to see Prime Instant Videos in other categories.

7. Tap All to view all videos, or tap Prime to view videos eligible for free streaming with a Prime membership.

8. Scroll down to see more categories of movies and TV shows for instant streaming, rental, or purchase.

Viewing Movie Details

The Movie Details screen provides viewing options, production information, and the duration of the movie. You might also find a plot overview and reviews of the film.

1. Tap a movie title in the Video Store.

2. Tap Watch Trailer to see the movie trailer.

3. Tap the name of the director to find other films he or she has made.

4. View the duration of the video.

5. View the rental terms if you choose to rent the movie.

6. Tap Rental & Purchase Details to view information about rental and purchase agreements from Amazon.

7. Scroll down to see recommended titles based on what other customers purchased and read customer reviews of the movie.

X-Ray for Movies

If a movie takes advantage of Amazon's new X-Ray for Movies feature, it's noted in the upper-right corner of the Movie Details screen. I cover this tool in more detail later in this chapter.

Renting or Purchasing a Movie

You can rent or purchase a movie on your Kindle Fire. A rental enables you to view the movie for a short period of time for a low price, similar to renting a movie from a RedBox kiosk. Purchasing a movie is more expensive, but you can watch the movie whenever you want without time restrictions, as when you purchase a movie at a retail store.

1. From the movie details screen, tap the price to rent or purchase the movie.

2. Tap the green Rent or Purchase button to complete your transaction.

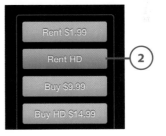

Standard vs. High Definition

If you have a Kindle Fire HD (either the 7-inch or the 8.9-inch unit), rent or purchase the HD (high-definition) format to take full advantage of your device's display. The HD format is more expensive, but it's worth it.

If you have a base Kindle Fire model, you can rent or purchase the standard-definition format of the movie if you will be viewing the movie only on your Kindle Fire. If you have an HD-TV or other device, however, you might still want to purchase the HD format so you can watch it in higher quality on those devices. HD videos play fine on your Kindle Fire; they just display in SD.

It's Not All Good

Rented Movies Might Expire Sooner Than You Think

When you rent a movie, it typically expires 24 or 48 hours after you start watching it. However, if you initiate a download of the video to your Kindle Fire, that also starts the clock on the expiration period. Therefore, if you download a video to your Kindle Fire, pay careful attention to the expiration of the rental.

When you initiate a download, Amazon displays a notification informing you that you are about to start the rental period and telling you how many hours you have to watch the movie.

Viewing TV Show Details

Amazon carries hundreds of television shows, from sitcoms to miniseries.

1. Tap a TV show in the Video Store.

2. Scroll to see available seasons.

3. Scroll down to see additional information.

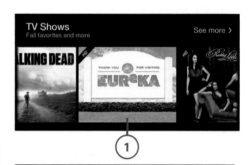

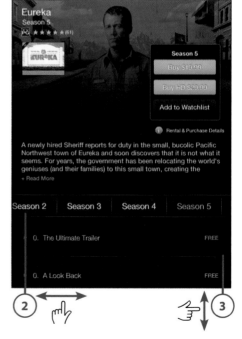

4. Tap an episode to see details on that episode.

5. Scroll down to see additional series details.

6. Tap the network name to see more TV shows from that network.

7. Scroll to see TV shows other customers bought.

8. Read reviews of the series from other customers.

9. Scroll to see the cast and other information about the series.

10. Tap a cast member's name to get more information about that person's career from the preinstalled IMDb app.

Missing Additional Show Details

Some movies and TV shows provide more information on their detail screens than others. If a listing falls short, you can always look up more information about a movie or TV show using the Silk browser on your Kindle Fire.

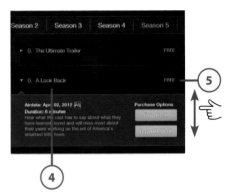

Buying TV Shows by Episode

Amazon offers the capability to purchase either single episodes or entire seasons of TV shows. Single episodes of a TV show are handy if you missed an episode of a favorite show on TV.

1. Tap a TV show from the Video Store.

2. Select a season.

3. Tap the episode you want to purchase.

4. Tap the price to purchase the episode.

5. Tap the green Buy button to complete your purchase.

No TV Show Rentals

Unlike movies, TV shows are not available as rentals. You can purchase a TV show (either a single episode or an entire series) or stream a TV show if it's currently available through Amazon Prime Instant Video.

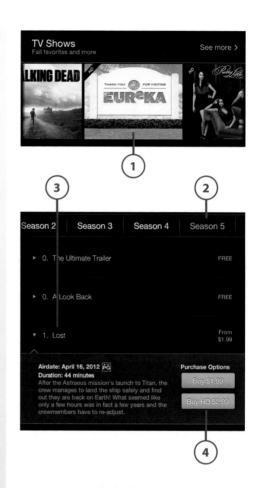

Purchasing Complete TV Show Seasons

If you're catching up on previous seasons or want to complete your collection of a TV series, you can save a little money by purchasing the entire season at once.

1. Tap a TV show from the Video Store.

2. Tap the price to purchase the season.

3. Tap the green Buy button to complete your purchase.

Purchasing a TV Show from Prime Instant Video

You can stream a TV show from Prime Instant Video, but if you want to download it to your device so you can watch without a Wi-Fi connection, you need to purchase it.

1. Tap a TV show from the Prime Instant Video listing.

2. Tap a season.

3. To purchase the complete season, tap Purchase Options.

4. Tap the Buy option.

5. If you change your mind, tap Close.

6. To purchase a single episode, tap the name of the episode.

7. Tap Additional Purchase Options.

8. Tap the Buy option.

9. If you change your mind, tap Close.

Not Everything Is in HD

Some TV shows, such as early seasons of *Doctor Who,* are available in only one format. If a TV show is for sale in multiple formats, the purchase options reflect those choices.

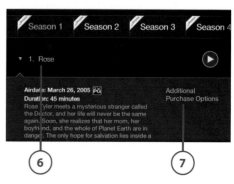

Buying a Season TV Pass

Amazon offers a "TV Pass" for some series. When you purchase a TV Pass, you immediately get the season's episodes that have already aired, and new episodes of the season are made available to you after they air, often the next day. Although you can view episodes on your Kindle Fire, TV Pass purchases must be made on the Amazon website through a browser.

1. In your web browser, go to www.amazon.com/Instant-Video to access the Video Store.

2. Click TV to browse all the available options.

3. Search for a particular series.

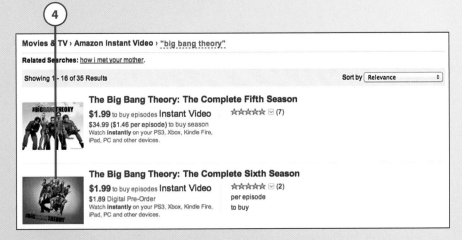

4. Click a current season of a series.

5. Click Buy TV Pass.

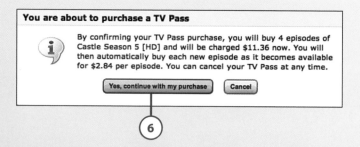

6. Click Yes, Continue with My Purchase.

Locating Your TV Pass Videos

Previously aired episodes of a series are immediately added to your Videos library. You can access them from Your Video Library on the Amazon site (www.amazon.com/gp/video/library) or from the Videos library on your Kindle Fire. New episodes automatically appear in your Videos library as they become available.

You can cancel a TV Pass at any time. If you decide to cancel a series, go to Your Video Library on the Amazon site. Click Passes and Preorders, and then click Cancel TV Pass.

Working with Your Video Library

Your video library contains video items that you own, as well as video rentals from the Video Store. Items that you own are always available in your video library unless you permanently delete them. Items that you rent appear in your video library only during the rental period, after which time they disappear.

Your Video Library

You can delete videos from your video library by visiting the Your Video Library page at www.amazon.com/gp/video/library. Simply click a video and then click the Delete link.

Watching a Movie or TV Show

You can stream movies and TV episodes from the cloud to your Kindle Fire as long as you have an active Wi-Fi connection. You can also watch videos that you've downloaded to your device.

1. From the Videos screen, tap Library.

2. Tap Movies or TV to locate the video you want to watch.

3. Tap Cloud to see movies in the cloud, or tap Device to see videos you've downloaded.

4. Tap the Menu button to bring up other options.

5. Tap Sort By to change how your videos are sorted, either by Recent or by Title.

6. Tap a video you want to watch.

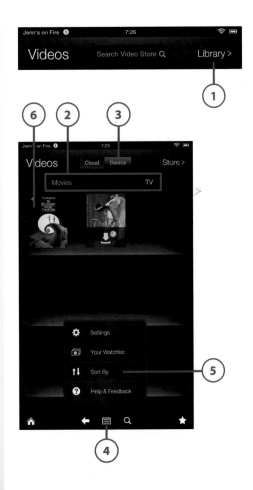

7. Tap Watch Now to watch the video. You must remain connected to Wi-Fi while watching if you're streaming from the cloud.

8. Tap Download if you choose to download the video so that you can watch it even when you're not connected to Wi-Fi.

9. If the video is a rental, a warning appears to notify you that the rental period is beginning. Tap Start Rental to proceed.

10. While a video is playing, tap the middle of the screen to display the controls.

11. Tap Play/Pause to pause or resume the video.

12. Drag the slider to move to a specific point in the video.

13. Tap the Skip Back button to move backward 10 seconds.

14. Drag the volume slider to adjust the volume.

15. Tap the left side of the volume slider to mute the audio.

16. Tap the right side of the volume slider to increase the audio to the maximum setting.

17. Tap the X-Ray info to get more details about an actor in a scene.

18. Tap Back to return to the details screen for the video.

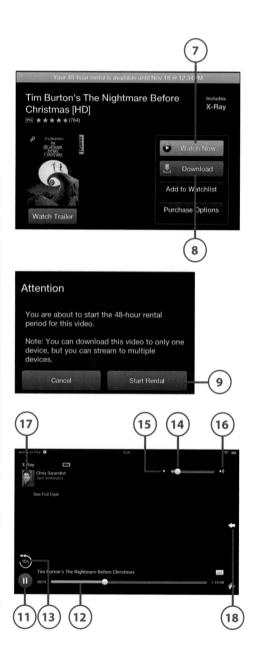

>>>Go Further

WATCHING AMAZON VIDEOS ON YOUR TV

After you rent or purchase a video, you can watch it on your Kindle Fire, your computer, or any compatible Internet-connected device. This includes your video game machine, Blu-ray player, Apple TV, or Internet-connected television. If you have an Amazon Prime account, you can also stream Amazon Instant Video titles over these devices.

You can also use a mini-HDMI cable to connect your Kindle Fire to your television and mirror your display on the TV.

Kindle Lending Library vs. Amazon Instant Video

Unlike the Kindle Lending Library for books, which can be utilized only directly from a Kindle device (not just any Kindle app), you can access Amazon Instant Video from your computer or other devices if you have an Amazon Prime account.

Using X-Ray for Video

Have you ever watched a movie and noticed a familiar actor, but you can't remember where you've seen him? X-Ray for Video tells you which actors are in each scene of a movie. If you want to learn more about an actor, you can get that person's complete film biography from IMDb, the Internet Movie Database.

1. While watching a movie, tap the middle of the screen to bring up the video controls.

2. View the X-Ray for Video information on the screen.

3. Tap an actor's name to get more information.

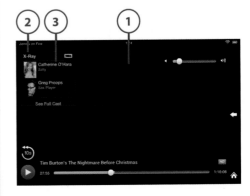

4. Scroll to see more information about the actor.

5. Scroll to access other films in which the actor appears.

6. Tap and hold a film you want to remember to view in the future.

7. Tap Add to Watchlist.

8. Tap See Full Cast for a complete cast listing for the movie.

9. Tap Close to return to your movie.

Adding a Video to Your Watchlist

As you browse the Video Store, you're likely to find more movies and TV shows than you can possibly watch in one sitting. Instead of purchasing them all at once, add them to your Watchlist so you remember them later.

1. From the Video Store, tap a movie or TV show that interests you.

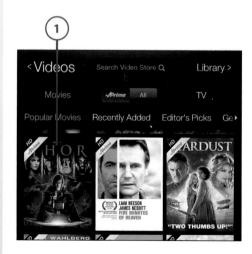

2. Tap Add to Watchlist.

3. Tap the Menu button.

4. Tap Your Watchlist.

Your Watchlist in the Video Store

Your Watchlist also appears on the main screen of the Video Store.

5. Tap Movies to view the movies in your Watchlist.

6. Tap TV to view the TV shows in your Watchlist.

7. Tap Prime to see videos on your Watchlist that are currently available for free streaming.

8. Tap a movie or TV show on your Watchlist to open the details screen.

Removing a Video from Your Watchlist

You can remove a video from your Watchlist by tapping the movie or TV show and then tapping the Remove from Watchlist button.

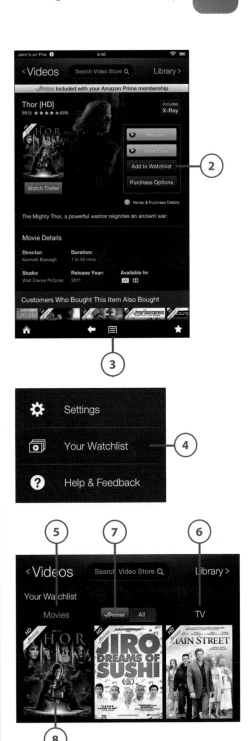

Downloading Movies

If you want to watch a video on a car trip, plane flight, or someplace else where you cannot get Wi-Fi access, you can plan ahead and download the video to your device in advance.

1. From your Videos library, tap Cloud.

2. Tap Movies.

3. Tap and hold the movie you want to download.

4. Tap Download to download the movie to your device.

5. Watch the progress bar while the movie downloads.

6. When the movie has finished downloading, an icon appears on its thumbnail.

Managing Your Storage Space

Keep in mind that the average HD-quality movie is about 2GB, and the Kindle Fire HD comes with 16 or 32GB of storage (up to 64GB on the high-end models). By contrast, Amazon provides unlimited cloud storage for your Amazon purchases. It's best to store the majority of your movies in the cloud and download what you need only when you need it.

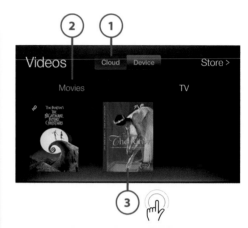

Downloading a TV Show

The process for downloading a TV show differs slightly from the process for movies because TV episodes are grouped by show.

1. From your Videos library, tap Cloud.

2. Tap TV.

3. Tap the TV show you want to download.

4. Tap the download icon for the episode you want to download.

5. Select the format you want to download. If you have a base-model Kindle Fire, choose SD format. If you have a Kindle Fire HD, you can choose HD for higher quality or choose SD to save time and storage.

6. Follow the progress of your download.

7. When the TV show has finished downloading, a check mark replaces the Download icon.

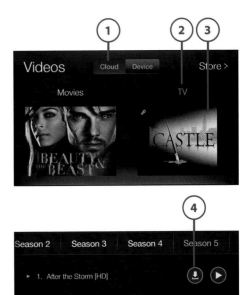

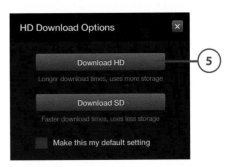

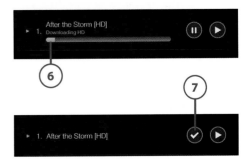

Removing a Downloaded Video

After you've watched a video, you might want to remove it from your device so that it doesn't take up space. If you own the video, you can download it again at any time.

1. From your Videos library, tap Device.

2. Tap and hold the video you want to delete from your device.

3. Tap Delete Download.

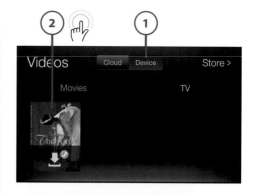

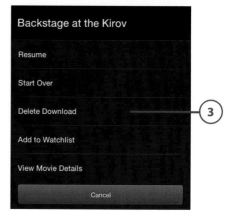

Sideloading Videos

Digital video comes in a wide assortment of formats. The Kindle Fire supports only one of them, MP4 (or MPEG 4). If you have video in other formats that you want to play on your Kindle Fire, you can convert it to an MP4 video using an app such as Handbrake on your PC or Mac. This free application and others like it convert into MP4 format any video that you download from the Internet or rip from DVDs.

Copying Video to Your Kindle Fire

Sideload videos onto your Kindle Fire using the instructions in Chapter 2, "Loading Your Kindle Fire."

1. Connect your Kindle Fire to your computer using a micro-USB cable.

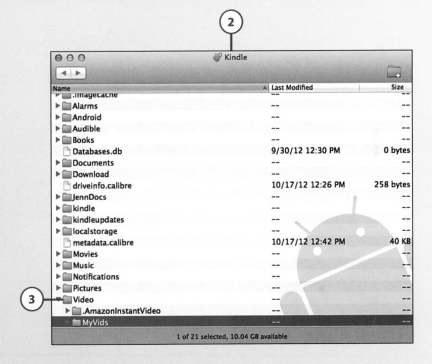

2. On a PC, open the drive for your Kindle Fire in Windows Explorer. On a Mac, open the Android File Transfer app.

3. Copy your video into the Video folder.

Organizing Your Personal Videos

You can create folders to organize your personal videos within the Kindle Fire's file system, but these folders do not appear when you view your videos on your Kindle Fire. The best use of a folder within the Video folder is simply to help distinguish your personal videos from any downloaded video content on your device.

Watching Sideloaded Videos

Sideloaded videos don't show up in your Videos library, even though they are stored in the Video folder. Instead, you need to use the Personal Video app on your Kindle Fire to watch them.

1. From your Home screen, tap Apps.

2. Tap the Personal Videos app.

3. Tap the video you want to watch.

4. Tap the middle of the screen to access the video controls.

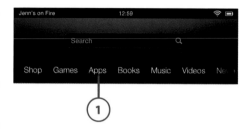

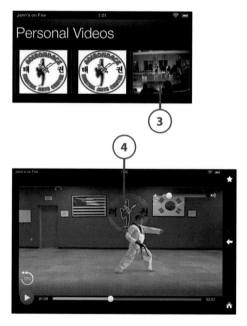

Deleting Sideloaded Videos

To delete sideloaded videos, you can simply delete the files from your Kindle Fire's Video folder using Windows Explorer (PC) or the Android File Transfer app (Mac). You can also delete them from within the Personal Videos app.

1. In Personal Videos, tap and hold the video you want to delete.

2. Tap Delete.

3. Tap OK to confirm the deletion.

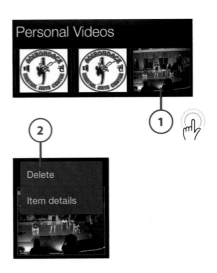

Turn your Kindle Fire
into a game machine

Get cool apps to enhance
the capabilities of your
Kindle Fire

In this chapter, you learn how to find and install apps from Amazon's Appstore for Android, as well as how to manage and use those apps. Topics include the following:

→ The Appstore
→ Your Apps library
→ Application Settings
→ Indispensable apps
→ Games for your Kindle Fire

8

Installing and Using Apps

You already know that your Kindle Fire is great for reading books, listening to music, and watching video. What you might not realize is that the Kindle Fire is capable of running apps that do a whole lot more. Your Kindle Fire comes with several apps already installed, and it provides access to Amazon's Appstore for Android so that you can get others. Apps that are available from the Appstore for Android on your Kindle Fire have been tested for compatibility with the Kindle Fire.

The Appstore for Android contains a wide assortment of apps for cooking, education, health and fitness, reference, productivity, shopping, sports, and games. Some of these apps are free; some are not. Unfortunately, you can't return an app for a refund after you buy it, so it's a good idea to read the reviews and look at the screenshots to decide whether an app is a good fit for you before you purchase it.

The Appstore

You purchase new apps for your Kindle Fire in the Appstore. When you browse the store from your Kindle Fire, all the apps listed are compatible with your device.

Appstore for Android from a Web Browser

You can also access the Appstore for Android on the Amazon website (www.amazon.com) on your computer using a web browser, but not all of the apps you see listed are compatible with your Kindle Fire. When you view an app from the Appstore for Android on a web browser, look for a check mark for the Kindle Fire, which indicates that the app is compatible.

An app compatible with the Kindle Fire.

Browsing Apps

The Appstore offers several tools to make shopping for apps easier.

1. From the Home screen, tap Apps to enter the Appstore.

2. Amazon offers a paid app for free every day. Tap to install the app.

3. Scroll to view highly rated apps.

4. Scroll to view apps that Amazon has recommended for you based on your previous browsing and purchasing history.

5. Scroll down to see new apps.

6. Tap to look for apps by category.

Returning to the Appstore

After you've opened the Apps library for the first time, tapping Apps from the Home screen puts you in the Apps library instead of the Appstore. To access the Appstore from the Apps library, tap Store at the top of the page.

Viewing and Purchasing Apps

You can view details of an app before you decide to purchase it.

1. Tap an app that interests you.

2. Scroll to view screenshots of the app.

3. Read a description of the app.

4. Scroll down to read reviews from other customers. You can also add your own review of the app.

5. Scroll down and read the permissions the app requires. These might have an impact on your privacy.

6. Read the product details, including the file size of the app, so you can control your storage.

7. Tap the price to purchase and install the app. If the app is free, the price button reads Free.

8. Tap the Save for Later button if you're interested in the app but not ready to purchase yet.

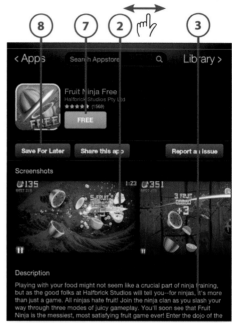

TEST-DRIVING AN APP

>>>Go Further

Most apps force you to make a purchasing decision based on a description, screenshots, and reviews. Some apps, however, offer a "test drive" mode on the Appstore for Android website. Use the web browser on your computer to go to the Appstore for Android, and then click the Test Drive Apps option. Choose an app to test. The app opens in a pop-up window with a replica of an Android device. Test drives are time-limited, and not all features might be available, but they generally offer a good idea of what the app has to offer. Remember to check whether the app is compatible with your Kindle Fire before purchasing from the Web.

Viewing Saved or Recently Viewed Apps

Your Saved for Later list is a wish list for apps. You can add to this list and access it at any time.

1. From anywhere in the Appstore, tap the menu icon.

2. Tap Saved for Later to view apps you've saved.

3. Tap an app in your list to open the details screen in the Appstore, where you can read more about it and purchase it if you're ready.

Removing Items from the Saved for Later List

Apps remain in the Saved for Later list until you remove them, even if you purchase the app. To remove an app from the list, tap it to open the details screen and then tap the Saved button.

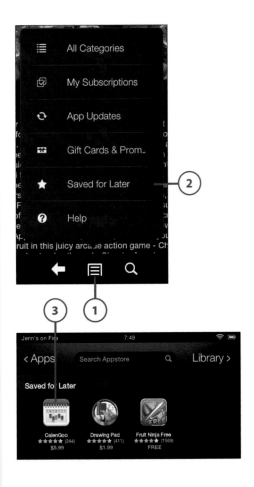

Viewing Subscriptions

Some magazines are available for the Kindle Fire as apps. For example, the magazines *WIRED* and *The New Yorker* both have apps for accessing their content. The apps might offer additional features that aren't available from the Kindle Fire Newsstand. These magazines are typically offered as a free app, but to read the content, you must subscribe via the app. You can view the status and manage these subscriptions from the Appstore.

1. From the Appstore, tap the menu icon.

2. Tap My Subscriptions.

3. Tap a subscription to view details about it.

4. Tap Change Subscription Period if you want to change from a monthly subscription to an annual basis.

5. Tap a new subscription period.

6. Tap Save Changes.

7. If you want to turn off autorenewal so that your subscription is not automatically renewed when it's due to expire, tap Turn Off Auto-Renewal.

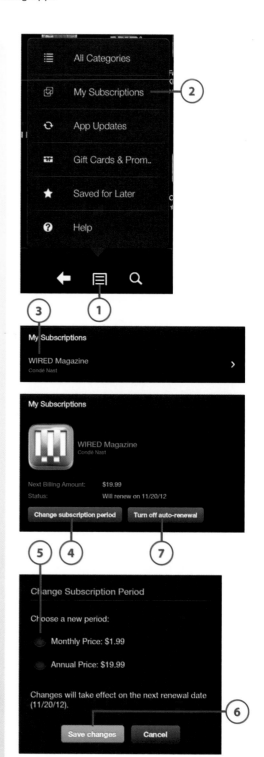

8. Tap Turn off Auto-Renewal.

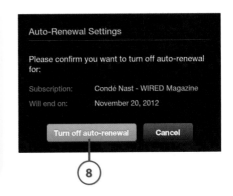

8

Reactivating Auto-Renewal

After you've turned off auto-renewal, you can turn it back on by tapping Turn On Auto-Renewal in the subscription details.

Your Apps Library

Your Apps library contains applications that you have downloaded to your device, as well as applications that you have purchased but not downloaded. When you purchase an app from the Appstore directly on your Kindle Fire, the app is added to your Apps library and installed on your device.

Included Free Apps

Amazon includes some free apps in your Apps library, but not all of them are preinstalled on your Kindle Fire. You'll see them when you tap the Cloud tab in your Apps library.

Browsing Your Apps Library

All your apps are available by browsing your Apps library.

1. From the Home screen, tap Apps. The Appstore opens.

2. Tap Library.

1

2

3. Tap Cloud to see all the apps you've purchased, both on your device and in the cloud.

4. Tap Device to see only the apps that are installed on your device.

5. Tap By Recent to sort your apps according to when they were added to your library.

6. Tap By Title to sort your apps by title.

7. Scroll to see more apps.

8. Tap the Search icon to search your Apps library.

Installing a Purchased App

When you purchase an app from the Appstore for Android using your web browser, the app is stored in the cloud. You need to download and install it before you can use it. Installed apps appear in the Cloud listing with a check mark.

1. From the Cloud list in the Apps library, tap the app that you want to install.

2. Wait for your app to download and install. You can tap several apps at a time, and each is queued for download. A checkmark appears on the icon when the app is downloaded.

3. Tap an app to open it.

Accessing Your Apps

Aside from the Apps library, newly installed apps appear on the Carousel on your home screen.

It's Not All Good

Installing Apps from Unknown Sources

Your Kindle Fire provides the capability to sideload third-party apps from sources other than the Appstore. However, I advise against doing so, for a couple reasons. First, many of the apps I tested crashed my Kindle Fire or caused unpredictable behavior. The Kindle Fire version of the Android operating system is highly customized, so features that work well on an Android phone or tablet might not work on the Kindle Fire. Second, Android apps are a common source of Android viruses, and because the Kindle Fire is directly tied to your Amazon account, the risk of installing apps from unkown sources is simply too great to ignore.

Adding an App to Favorites

You can add an app to your Favorites shelf for easier access. Find more information on using and organizing your Favorites in Chapter 1, "Getting Started with the Kindle Fire."

1. Tap Device to see only the apps that you've installed.

2. Tap and hold the app that you want to add to Favorites.

3. Tap Add to Favorites.

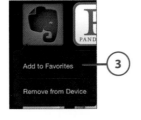

Uninstalling an App

Uninstalling an app removes it from your device, but it remains stored in the cloud. You can reinstall the app later without having to pay for it again.

1. Tap Device to see only the apps you've installed.

2. Tap and hold the app that you want to uninstall.

3. Tap Remove from Device to uninstall the app.

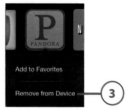

Cannot Uninstall Preinstalled Apps

Contacts, E-mail, Help & Feedback, IMDb, OfficeSuite, Personal Videos, Shop Amazon, Silk, and Calendar are all preinstalled apps that you cannot uninstall from your Kindle Fire. Each of these apps serves a purpose on the device. For example, the X-Ray for Movies feature uses IMDb.

Updating an Application

Your Kindle Fire automatically updates apps as new versions are released. You can change your update settings to turn off automatic updates or to receive a notice when an app is updated.

1. Swipe down from the status bar to open Settings.

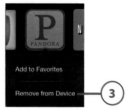

2. Tap More.

3. Tap Applications.

4. Tap Appstore.

5. Tap Automatic Updates.

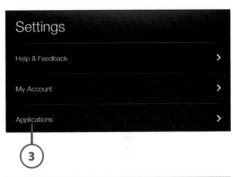

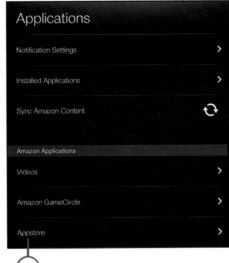

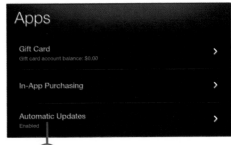

6. Enable Automatic Updates is selected by default. Deselect this option if you don't want your Kindle Fire to update apps automatically.

7. Tap Notify Me When Updates Are Installed if you want your Kindle Fire to display a notification whenever a new version of an app is installed. Notifications appear in the status bar.

Application Settings

Apps are prone to bugs that can cause them to become unresponsive or crash. This is why apps get updated so often, to fix the problems that become obvious only when a large number of users interact with the app.

In some cases, you might need to force an application to close if it's misbehaving. If an app is behaving unpredictably even after you force-close it and relaunch it, the app might have some corrupted data in its cache or database. You can force-close apps and delete app data from the Application Settings screen.

Force-Stopping an Application

If an app is causing problems on your Kindle Fire, or if it hangs and becomes unresponsive, you can force the app to close. This is called *force-stopping* an app.

1. Swipe down from the status bar.

2. Tap More.

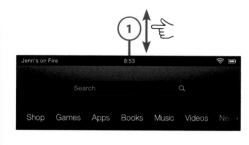

3. Tap Applications.

4. Tap Installed Applications.

5. Scroll to locate the app you want to stop, and then tap the app that's frozen.

6. Tap Force Stop to stop the app.

7. Tap OK in the confirmation dialog box to force-stop the app.

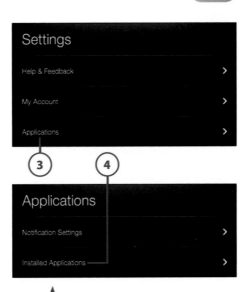

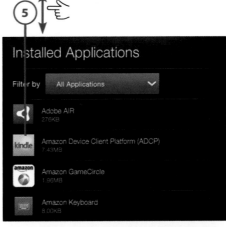

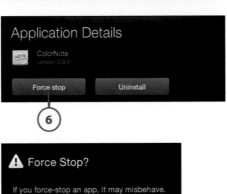

SHOULD YOU CLOSE YOUR APPS?

When you finish with an app on your Kindle Fire, you tap the Home button to get back to the home screen. When you do this, the app remains running in the background. After awhile, you might have dozens of apps running in the background on your Kindle Fire.

On a laptop or desktop computer, you don't want to have a large number of applications running when you're not using them because they can slow your computer. However, the Kindle Fire's operating system is designed to account for many apps running that aren't currently in use. When you switch away from an app, it enters a state in which it doesn't do anything. Some apps are designed to periodically check for content or perform some other task, but they go back to sleep after that task is completed. So although you can close apps you're not using, it's unnecessary.

Clearing Application Data

If an app is not working properly even after you force-stop it, the app's data might be corrupt. You can clear an app's data in Application settings.

1. While viewing the Installed Application settings, tap the app whose data you want to clear.

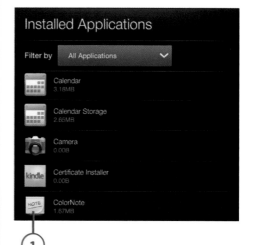

2. Tap Clear Data.

3. Tap OK in the confirmation dialog box.

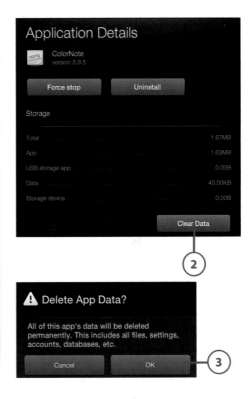

It's Not All Good

Clearing Data Clears Everything

When you clear data for an app, you clear all settings and any other data that the app has stored. The next time you launch the app, it starts with the default settings. Don't clear data unless you're sure that you don't need any information that the app is storing.

Indispensable Apps

Amazon includes several apps on your Kindle Fire when it ships. Some of these, such as the E-mail app, you might use every day. Other apps available in the Appstore are equally indispensable. These are merely my recommendations; you'll undoubtedly develop your own list of must-have apps as you use your Kindle Fire.

Evernote

Evernote is a notetaking app that enables you to store notes, photos, lists, and all the other scraps of data that cross your path. You can share notebooks with your computer, your smartphone, and even other Evernote users.

1. Launch Evernote.

2. Sign in or create a new Evernote account.

3. Add a new note.

4. Enter a note title.

5. Enter the note's content.

6. Add tags, audio, and photos to the note.

7. Tap Done to save the note.

8. Create different notebooks to organize your ideas.

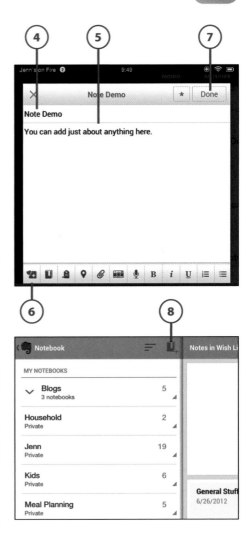

Pandora

Pandora Internet Radio is a service that enables you to enter the name of a song or artist to get recommendations from Pandora for other songs you'll almost certainly like. It's a great way to discover new music.

1. Launch Pandora.

2. Sign in or create a new Pandora account.

3. To create a new station, enter an artist, genre, or composer. You can also view existing stations sorted by genre.

4. While a station is playing, tap Pause to pause playback. Tap Play to resume.

5. Tap Next to skip to a new song.

6. Tap the thumbs-up to tell Pandora that you like the current song.

7. Tap the thumbs-down to tell Pandora that you don't like the current song and to skip to the next song.

8. Tap the menu icon to see more options.

9. Tap Buy Track if you want to purchase the current song or album. This takes you to the Music Store on your Kindle Fire to complete the transaction.

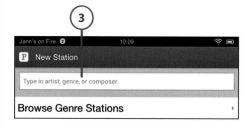

It's Not All Good

Finding Ads in Your Apps

Many free apps, such as Pandora, are ad supported. You get to use the app for free, but in return, you're presented with ads on the screen. Some apps offer an upgrade to an ad-free version, for a price. If the ads are unobtrusive, you hardly notice them after awhile. In the case of an app such as Pandora, however, with static ads displaying on the screen during every song and video ads appearing after every other song, upgrading is well worth the price if you use the app frequently.

ES File Explorer

The ES File Explorer app provides a convenient way to view files that are stored on your Kindle Fire. It's the easiest way I've found to locate files you downloaded from the Internet, attachments you've saved from e-mails, and other files stored on your Kindle Fire's internal memory.

Be Careful When Deleting or Renaming Files

Because ES File Explorer enables you to see the files that are part of your Kindle Fire's operating system, it's possible for you to corrupt your Kindle Fire if you delete or rename a system file. Be careful!

1. Launch ES File Explorer.

2. Tap a folder to see the contents of the folder.

3. Tap a file to open it, and then select an app capable of viewing it.

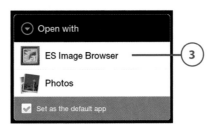

ES File Explorer and Viewing Files

ES File Explorer includes ES Image Browser and other mini-apps that can view certain file types. If you attempt to open a file type in ES File Explorer that isn't supported on your Kindle Fire, ES File Explorer typically displays a black screen instead of the file. In these cases, just tap Back to return to the interface.

Go Further

MORE APPS FOR YOUR CONSIDERATION

With more than 10,000 apps in the Appstore, this chapter could be endless. Other apps I use that you might want to explore include Weather+, Netflix, CalenGoo, Timers4Me, iTranslate, Pinterest, and Pocket (formerly Read It Later).

Games for Your Kindle Fire

No tablet device is complete without games, and the Kindle Fire is no exception. You can purchase and install games on your Kindle Fire from the Appstore for Android. They appear in the Apps library along with all your other apps.

Games also appear in the Games library. This screen makes it faster to access your games and provides access to certain game-specific features, such as tracking achievements and comparing scores with your friends using GameCircle.

Is GameCircle Necessary?

GameCircle adds a social element to your gameplay, but if that's not your thing, it's easily ignored. Learn more about GameCircle in Chapter 9, "Using Social Media and Chat."

Accessing Games

The Games library contains all apps that the Kindle Fire identifies as games. Developers identify the category of an app when they submit it to the Appstore.

1. From the home screen, tap Games.

2. Tap to download and install the app if it hasn't already been installed, or tap to play the game.

3. Tap Store to enter a special area in the Appstore for games.

4. Scroll to locate a game.

5. Choose a category of games to hone in on what you like to play.

6. Tap a game to view the details page.

7. Tap the price to purchase the game. This button reads Free if there is no charge for the app.

8. Tap Get App.

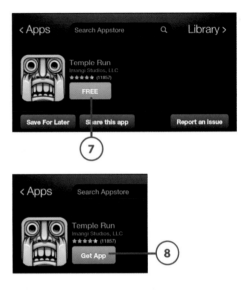

GAME RECOMMENDATIONS

Every game enthusiast has a favorite type of games. If you enjoy action games, try Temple Run, Fruit Ninja, and Doodle Jump. If you like physics-based games, any variation of Angry Birds fits the bill. Mystery Manor is a hidden-object game that's constantly expanding. If you want to play turn-based social games with your friends, consider Draw Something or Words with Friends. The Appstore has several sudoku apps for puzzle enthusiasts, or try Unblock Me. If you're feeling nostalgic for the board games of your youth, download The Game of Life.

>>>Go Further

Make video calls

Update your
Facebook status

Compare game
scores with
your friends

→ Sharing with Facebook, Twitter, and the Kindle community
→ Video chatting over Skype
→ Sharing game achievements with GameCircle

Using Social Media and Chat

Your Kindle Fire provides several ways for you to connect with friends and family. Share notes, highlights, and final thoughts about the books you read on Facebook and Twitter. Import your Facebook photos onto your Kindle Fire. Make free video chat calls using the Skype app and the camera on your Kindle Fire. Compare achievements and high scores in your games with friends on GameCircle.

If you add some free apps to your Kindle Fire, you can also keep up with what your friends are doing on Facebook and Twitter.

Sharing with Facebook, Twitter, and the Kindle Community

When you initially set up your Kindle Fire, you are prompted to provide your Facebook and Twitter logins. Your Kindle Fire makes use of this information in several ways. Whenever you create a note or highlight in a book, you can quickly share it with your Facebook friends and Twitter followers.

Amazon also maintains its own social network, called the Kindle community. The Kindle community shares comments, reviews, and rankings of Kindle books.

It's Not All Good

Social Network Integration Does Not Equal Full Interaction

Adding your Facebook and Twitter information to your Kindle Fire settings enables you to post updates about your Kindle books but does not give you full access to Facebook and Twitter. If you want to post other updates or access your newsfeed, you need to download an app from the Appstore for Android. These apps are not preinstalled on the Kindle Fire.

Setting Up Your Social Networks

The initial setup sequence for your Kindle Fire asks for your Facebook and Twitter account information. If you did not provide that information initially, you can add it later.

1. Swipe down from the status bar.

2. Tap More from the settings options.

3. Tap My Account.

4. Tap Manage Social Network Accounts.

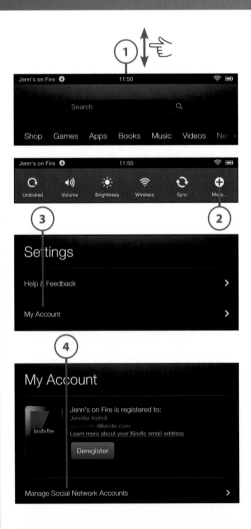

5. Tap Facebook if you want to link a Facebook account to your Kindle Fire.

6. Tap Log In. If you don't already have an account, tap Sign Up. Follow the prompts to authorize Amazon to link to your Facebook account.

7. Tap Twitter if you want to link a Twitter account to your Kindle Fire.

8. Enter your account info.

9. If you don't already have a Twitter account, tap Sign Up.

10. Tap Authorize App and then follow the prompts to authorize Amazon to link to your Twitter account.

11. After linking your accounts, you can unlink them, if necessary, by tapping Unlink.

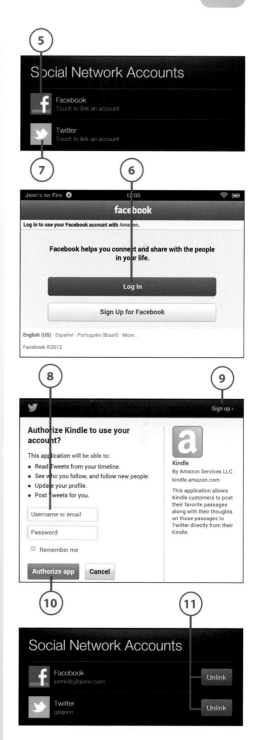

Sharing General Comments About Books

As you read a book on your Kindle Fire, you can share your thoughts with the Kindle community and your friends on Facebook and Twitter.

1. Tap the middle of a page in a book.

2. Tap Share.

3. Enter a comment.

4. Share with Twitter and Facebook, or choose just one of these services. Both services are selected by default if you have linked your Kindle Fire to those accounts.

5. Tap Share.

6. Your comment appears in the general thread for the book on the Kindle community. You can delete your comment by tapping the X button.

7. Scroll to read other readers' comments.

8. Press the Back button to return to your book.

Seeing Your Twitter and Facebook Posts

When you share your comments, you see the post as it appears in the Kindle community, but not your Facebook or Twitter updates. To see those, you need to access Facebook and Twitter. You can do this on your Kindle Fire using Silk to browse to the Facebook and Twitter sites or using a Facebook or Twitter app downloaded from the Appstore. You can also use a web browser on your computer.

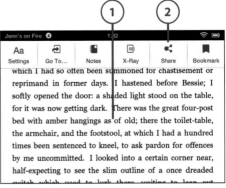

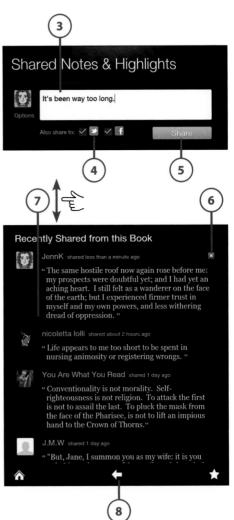

Sharing Highlights from Books

You can highlight key passages in a book to share with the Kindle community and your friends on Twitter and Facebook.

Adding Highlights

Learn how to mark up your books with highlights in the "Working with Notes and Highlights" section of Chapter 4, "Reading on the Kindle Fire."

1. In a book, tap and hold while moving over a passage to select it.

2. Tap Share.

3. Add an optional note.

4. Share with Twitter and Facebook, or choose just one of these services. Both services are selected by default if you have linked your Kindle Fire to those accounts.

5. Tap Share.

6. Press the Back button to return to your book.

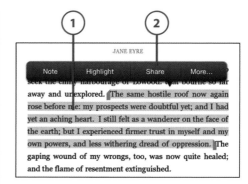

Go Further

THE KINDLE COMMUNITY

When you share highlights and notes, rate a book, or generally comment on a Kindle book, those insights are automatically posted to the Kindle community, as well as to Twitter or Facebook (if you opted to share with those services). To access more of the Kindle community and follow other readers with similar reading tastes, use your web browser to go to kindle.amazon.com.

Before You Go in Books

When you reach the end of a book, the Before You Go page appears. Rate and review the book you just read, and share your comments with the Kindle community, your Facebook friends, and your Twitter followers.

1. From the Before You Go page, tap Review This Book.

2. Tap the stars to give the book a rating.

3. Type a headline for your review.

4. Enter a review. Your review must be at least 20 words, but it can be quite lengthy, if you prefer.

5. Tap Submit.

6. Tap Share That You Have Finished Reading.

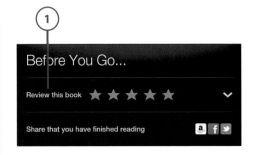

7. Enter your comments.

8. Share with Twitter and Facebook, or choose just one of these services. Both services are selected by default if you have linked your Kindle Fire to those accounts.

9. Tap Share.

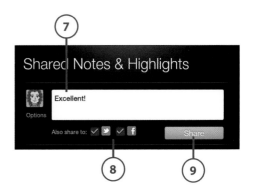

Importing Your Facebook Photos

If you linked your Facebook account to your Kindle Fire, you can import your Facebook photo gallery into the Photos library. Imported photos are stored in the cloud. You can then download them onto your device, if you want.

1. From the Home screen, tap Photos.

2. Tap the menu button.

3. Tap Import.

4. Tap OK to continue. It might take a minute for your import to begin.

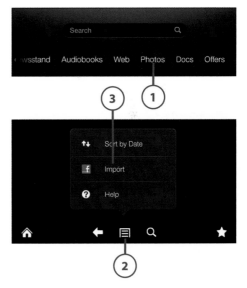

5. Tap OK to confirm the import.

6. The Kindle Fire imports your photos into the same folders in which they were organized on Facebook. Tap a folder to view the photos in that gallery.

Storing Photos on Your Cloud Drive

Imported Facebook photos are stored on your Cloud Drive. For more information about how to use your Cloud Drive, see the "Amazon Cloud Drive" section of Chapter 2, "Loading Your Kindle Fire." Remember, you have 5GB of free space on your Cloud Drive. If you're importing a lot of photos, purchase additional cloud storage, if necessary.

Using the Facebook App

If you want to post status updates or read your newsfeed on Facebook, you need to install a Facebook app. The Appstore offers several apps that can connect to Facebook, including the official Facebook app.

Downloading and Installing the Facebook App

To learn how to locate, download, and install an app from the Appstore for Android, see Chapter 8, "Installing and Using Apps."

1. Download and install the Facebook app from the Appstore, and then tap the app to open it.

2. The Facebook app automatically uses your account information if you linked your Facebook account to your Kindle Fire. Scroll down to read your newsfeed.

3. Tap the menu button to open the side menu.

4. Tap Messages to view your private messages.

5. Tap Events to respond to events to which you've been invited.

6. Tap Friends to access a list of all your Facebook friends and any pages you've Liked.

7. Tap a group to access the group's newsfeed.

8. Swipe from right to left to close the menu and return to your newsfeed.

9. Tap the Friends icon to respond to friend requests.

10. Tap the Messages icon to read and send private messages.

11. Tap the Notifications icon to view your notifications.

12. Tap Status to post a status update.

13. Tap Photo to upload a photo from your Photos library.

14. Tap the menu icon to access settings for the Facebook app.

Some Features Are Not for the Kindle Fire

The Facebook app is designed for all Android devices, including smartphones, so some of the features do not work on the Kindle Fire. The Check In feature cannot pinpoint your location, and most of the Settings options are designed for Android smartphone notifications, not the Kindle Fire.

>>>Go Further

USING TWITTER FROM YOUR KINDLE FIRE

At this time, no official Twitter app exists for the Kindle Fire. If you want to view your timeline and tweet from your Kindle Fire, you need to install a third-party app from the Appstore. Tweetcaster is a popular choice that displays your newsfeed, allows you to compose tweets, shows you trending topics, and enables you to manage your account and followers.

Some apps consolidate all your social media networks in one place. HootSuite connects to Twitter, Facebook, FourSquare, and LinkedIn. Seesmic accesses Twitter and Facebook. Scope, an app still in beta, brings together Facebook, Twitter, FourSquare, Instagram, and Tumblr.

Video Chatting over Skype

Your Kindle Fire has a front-facing camera to facilitate video chat. Skype is a free app that makes video calls to anyone around the world. Put the two together, and you have everything you need to video chat with your friends and family. You can also use it to make free voice calls to other Skype users or buy Skype credits to make regular domestic and international voice calls.

Skype is available for the Kindle Fire, other Android tablets and smartphones, iPhone and iPad, Windows, and Mac. If you want to video chat with someone, chances are, she can install the Skype app to facilitate it.

Setting Up Skype

Amazon adds the Skype account to your cloud account when you register your Kindle Fire, so it's already available for you to download and install.

1. From the Home screen, tap Apps.

2. Tap Cloud to access your apps in the cloud.

3. Tap Skype to download and install the app. After the app is installed, tap it again to open it.

4. Tap Continue. When asked to accepts Skype's terms and conditions, tap Accept.

5. If you've used Skype in the past, enter your Skype name and password; then tap Sign In.

6. If you are new to Skype, tap Create an Account.

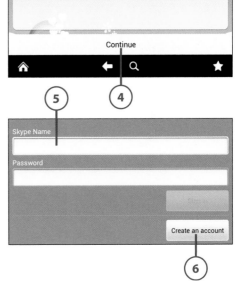

7. To sign up for an account, enter your contact information.

8. Tap Next. Tap Continue to progress through the information screens.

9. Tap Contacts to view and create Skype contacts.

10. Tap Call Phones to dial a number that's not in your contacts.

11. Tap Recent to call someone you've recently contacted.

12. Tap Profile to access your account information.

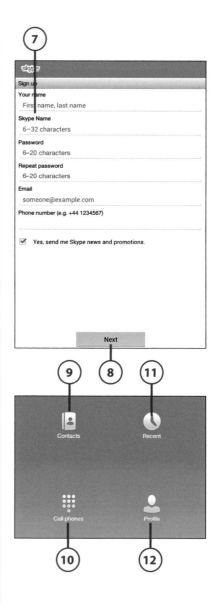

13. Tap Skype Credit to purchase credits to use on voice calls to landlines and mobile phones that don't have Skype.

14. Tap Skype Number to obtain a phone number where you can be reached by friends and family who do not have Skype.

15. Update your status for all your Skype contacts.

16. Tap Profile to add or edit your personal information, email address, location, and contact info.

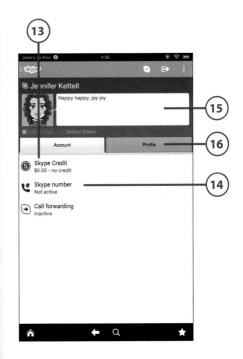

Adding Skype Contacts

Before making a call, add your friends and family to your Skype contacts list.

1. From the Skype home screen, tap Contacts.

2. Tap the menu button.

3. Tap Add Contacts.

4. Enter your friend's name, email address, or Skype name.

5. Tap the name you want to add.

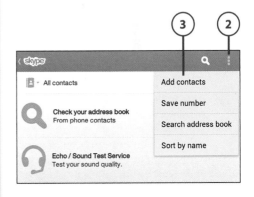

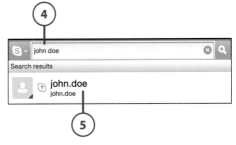

6. Tap Add.

7. Tap Add Contacts.

Making a Call with Skype

After your contact request has been accepted, tap the name of the contact to open that person's profile.

1. Tap Video Call to video chat.

2. Skype initiates a call. Tap the Disconnect button if the contact doesn't answer.

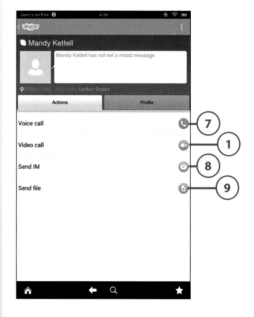

3. When the call connects, your contact's image appears. Tap the video camera to turn your own video image on or off.

4. Tap the microphone to mute the sound so that the person on the call can't hear you. Tap it again to restore the sound.

5. Tap the plus sign to add another caller to the video chat.

6. Tap the phone to disconnect the call.

7. Tap Voice Call to make a voice-only call.

8. Tap Send IM to send an instant message.

9. Tap Send File to send a file from your Docs, Videos, or Photos libraries.

10. To receive a call, tap the green phone button to respond only by voice.

11. Tap the green video camera to respond by voice and video.

12. Tap the red phone to reject the call.

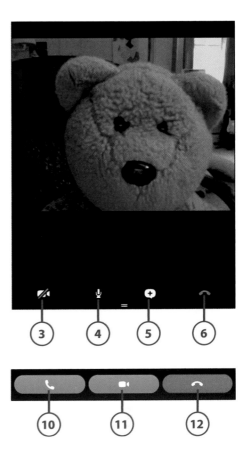

Sharing Game Achievements with GameCircle

Gaming on your Kindle Fire can become a social experience. Although you cannot play a multiplayer game on the Fire and interact with your friends in real time, you can share your achievements in certain games and challenge your friends to see who can get the highest score.

GameCircle brings this social interaction to your Kindle Fire games. Although you don't have to use GameCircle to play any game on the Kindle Fire, if you want to work to earn trophies or show up your friends, this is a great way to do it.

Identifying GameCircle Games

Not every game can interact with GameCircle. The game developer decides whether to include these features in an app.

1. From the Home screen, tap Games.

2. Tap Device to locate games that are installed on your Kindle Fire.

3. Select a game that shows a series of blue icons to the right of the name. These are GameCircle games.

4. Tap to see which GameCircle friends are playing this game.

5. Tap to see which achievements you've reached in the game.

6. Tap to see the leaderboard for the game.

7. Tap to see a summary for the game.

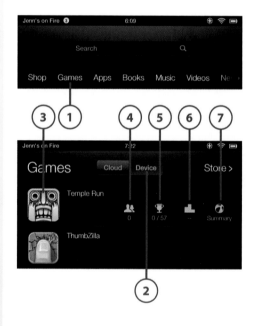

Buying and Installing Apps

If you need help finding and installing apps, see Chapter 8, "Installing and Using Apps."

It's Not All Good

Finding GameCircle Games

Locating GameCircle games is not easy. If you're shopping in the Appstore (whether from the Apps or Games pages), no designation in the game details lets you know whether a game is GameCircle enabled. You can tell only after you've installed downloaded the game and see the GameCircle details appear next to the game's listing in your Games library.

If you want to find out in advance whether a game utilizes GameCircle, you need to use a web browser to visit the Appstore for Android on the Amazon site. There you can click the Amazon GameCircle link to browse for games with this feature. Even on the website, however, the details page for the games themselves does not indicate whether they're powered by GameCircle. Let's hope that, as this feature becomes more popular, Amazon decides to promote it better.

Creating a GameCircle Profile

The first time you play a GameCircle-enabled game, your Kindle Fire automatically creates a nonsensical username and profile for you. Fortunately, you can update and customize it to your liking.

1. In the Games library, tap the menu icon.

2. Tap Profile to see your current GameCircle nickname and avatar.

3. Tap Edit.

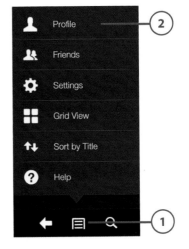

4. Swipe to choose a different avatar.

5. Tap to enter a new nickname.

6. Tap Update.

7. Tap the Back button to return to your Games library.

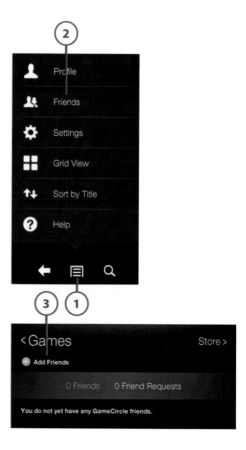

Adding Friends on GameCircle

Share your GameCircle nickname with your friends so they can find your name on the leaderboards.

1. From the Games library, tap the menu icon.

2. Tap Friends.

3. Tap Add Friends.

4. Enter the GameCircle nickname of a friend.

5. Tap the Search key.

6. When you find the friend you're looking for, tap Friend.

Accessing Game Achievements

Games in GameCircle offer trophies for achievments as you play. An achievement might be to collect a certain number of points or reach a particular level.

1. In the Games library, tap the trophy icon for a GameCircle game.

2. Scroll through the possible achivements.

3. Track your progress toward an achievement by viewing the completion percentage.

4. See the date when you completed a goal.

5. Tap Play to play the game.

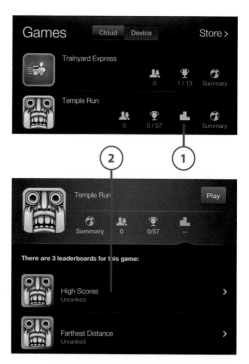

Accessing Leaderboards

The leaderboard shows current high scores for a game. Some games don't have a leaderboard; others have multiple leaderboards for different goals in the game.

1. In the Games library, tap the leaderboard icon for a GameCircle game.

2. Tap a leaderboard to see the gamers who have reached the top of that chart.

3. Tap Top 100 to see more rankings.

4. Tap a timeframe to see top scorers for that period.

5. Tap Play to play the game.

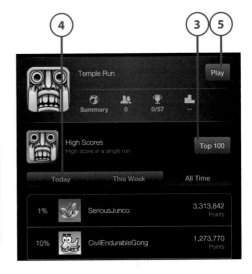

FINDING FRIENDS ON THE LEADERBOARDS

>>>Go Further

If you don't know anyone who plays games on a Kindle Fire, you can find GameCircle friends by checking the leaderboards for the games you play. Tap a nickname, and then tap Friend. The players with the highest scores are the most avid gamers and generally the most willing to make friends in a game.

Viewing Game Summaries

The game summary provides an overview of the leaderboards, achievements, and top players for a game.

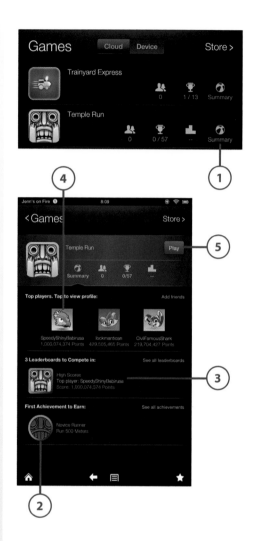

1. In the Games library, tap the Summary icon for a GameCircle game.

2. Review the next achievement you need to earn.

3. See how many points the high scorer has in the game.

4. Tap a top player's avatar to view that profile.

5. Tap Play to play the game.

Combine all
your accounts
into one inbox

Send and receive
attachments

Manage
multiple
e-mail
accounts

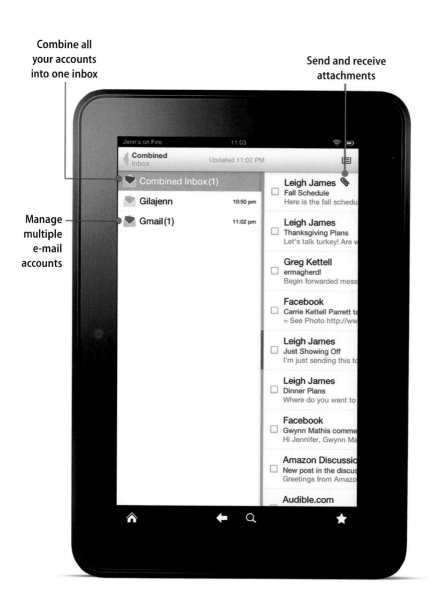

In this chapter, you learn how to set up e-mail accounts on your Kindle Fire, how to check your e-mail, and how to send e-mail. You also learn how to deal with e-mail attachments. Topics include the following:

→ E-mail accounts
→ Managing your e-mail inbox
→ Reading e-mail

Reading and Sending E-mail

Your Kindle Fire comes with an app for e-mail. You can read your e-mail, send mail, and even view attachments. The Kindle Fire supports various e-mail services, including Gmail, Hotmail, Yahoo!, and POP3 and IMAP servers.

E-mail Accounts

The first step in using e-mail on your Kindle Fire is setting up your e-mail account. You can set up multiple e-mail accounts on your Kindle Fire. You can then either access each inbox individually or use the combined inbox to see all your messages from all accounts on one screen.

Accessing the Add Account Page

The Kindle Fire makes adding your e-mail accounts easy, whether it's from a service such as Gmail, a Microsoft Exchange account, or a POP3/IMAP account.

1. Swipe down from the status bar to open the settings.

2. Tap More.

3. Tap Applications.

4. Tap E-mail, Contacts, Calendars.

5. Tap Add Account.

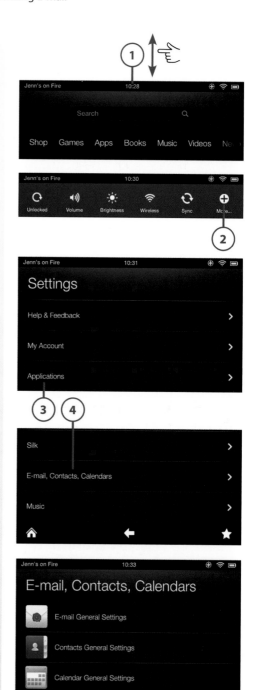

Adding a Gmail, Hotmail, AOL, or Yahoo! Account

If you have an account with a web-mail provider—Gmail, Hotmail, AOL, or Yahoo!—all you need is your e-mail address and password to set up your account on your Kindle Fire.

1. From the Add Account screen, tap the type of account you want to add.

2. Enter your name as you want it to appear on messages you send.

3. Enter your e-mail address. Use the full address, yourname@gmail.com (or yourname@aol.com, and so on).

4. Enter the password for your e-mail account.

5. Swipe down to continue.

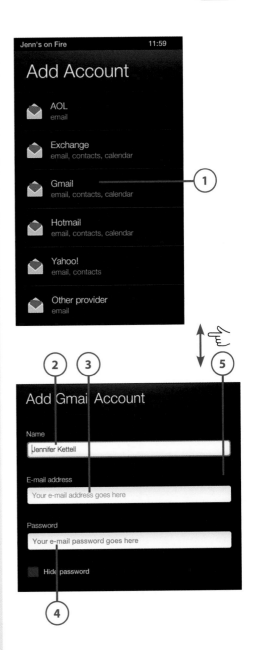

6. The Description field is automatically filled in with the name of the host, but you can change this. If you have more than one account with a host, you should customize this field to distinguish your account inboxes.

7. Tap Next.

8. If your host offers integration with a calendar or contact-management service, you can select to synchronize those with your Kindle Fire.

9. Tap Save.

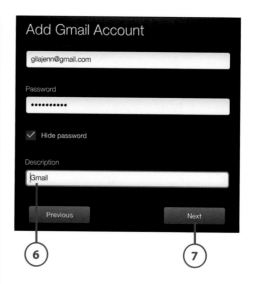

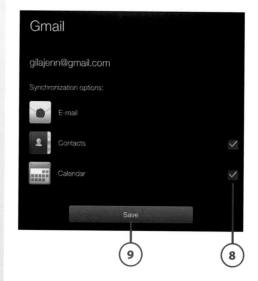

10. If you want to immediately access your e-mail, tap View Inbox.

11. To view or change your account settings, tap Go to Account Settings. (I talk more about this page in the "Modifying Your Account Settings" section.)

12. Tap Add Another Account if you have additional e-mail accounts.

13. Tap the Home button to return to your Home screen.

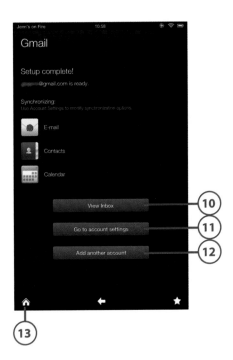

Using Your Contacts and Calendar

Many services enable you to synchronize the contacts and calendars you have stored on their site with your Kindle Fire's Contacts and Calendar apps. Learn more about these apps in Chapter 11, "Managing Your Personal Documents and Data."

Adding a POP3 or IMAP Account

If your e-mail account is through your Internet service provider (ISP) or a private domain, you need to gather more information before setting up your account. Be sure to have your e-mail address, password, IMAP or POP3 (incoming mail) server name, and SMTP (outgoing mail) server name. You also need to know what type of security is used on the mail servers (usually SSL).

1. From the Add Account screen, tap Other Provider.

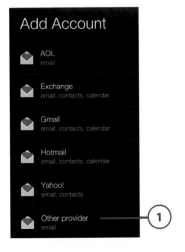

2. Type your name as you want it to appear on your messages.

3. Enter your e-mail address.

4. Type your password.

5. Swipe down to continue.

6. The Description field uses the domain name of your e-mail address by default. You can change this if you want.

7. Tap Next.

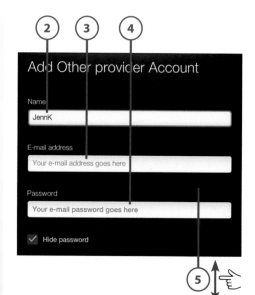

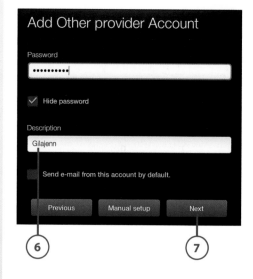

8. Choose an account type, either IMAP or POP3.

9. Confirm your username. This is usually your e-mail address, but if your host uses a different user-name, enter it here.

10. Confirm your password.

11. Swipe down to continue.

12. Enter your IMAP (or POP3) server name.

13. Select the security type of your server.

14. Change the port number, if neces-sary.

15. Swipe down to continue.

16. Enter your outgoing (SMTP) serv-er. In some cases, this is the same as the IMAP server name.

17. Select the security type for the SMTP server.

18. Change the port number, if neces-sary.

19. Swipe down to continue.

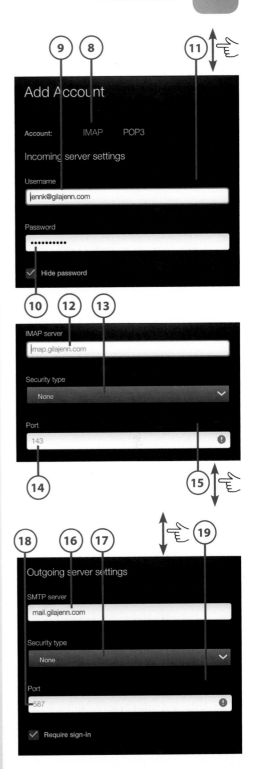

20. If your SMTP server requires you to log in, enter the username and password here.

21. Tap Next. If any of your settings has an error, you will not be able to move forward until you correct it.

22. Tap Save.

23. Tap View Inbox to immediately access your e-mail.

24. Tap Go to Account Settings to view or change your settings.

25. Tap Add Another Account if you have additional e-mail addresses you want to use with your Kindle Fire.

26. Tap the Home button to return to the Home screen.

Adding a Microsoft Exchange Account

If you use a Microsoft Exchange account, a type used in many corporate settings, you need to know your host server name and your domain name. If you don't know this information, ask your network administrator to help you set up your account.

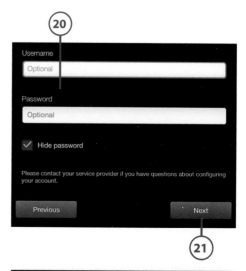

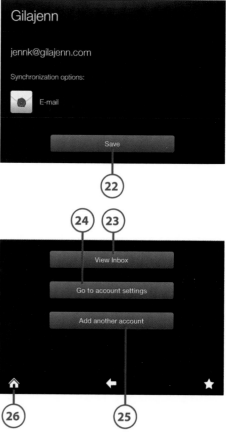

>>>Go Further

WHAT'S THE DIFFERENCE BETWEEN IMAP AND POP3?

The POP3 protocol downloads your e-mail onto your Kindle Fire (or your computer or other device). The advantage to this is that your e-mail is available even if you don't have an Internet connection. If you reply to a message, however, it is saved on your device, which means you cannot access it from your other computers and devices. And if your device crashes, your messages are lost. You can optionally configure POP3 to leave messages on the server, but if you read your mail on multiple devices, they are flagged as new on each device. Reading the same messages multiple times is sure to get annoying.

The IMAP protocol connects you directly to the server and keeps your e-mail on the server. This keeps it available from any device you use to access your mail, and all your replies remain available as well. Even if your device crashes, your messages are safe on the server. IMAP also lets you create folders to organize your messages. The only disadvantage to IMAP is that your mail is not available if you cannot connect to the Internet.

If your e-mail provider offers a choice of connecting to your e-mail server through either POP3 or IMAP, I recommend IMAP, especially if you're accessing your messages on multiple devices, such as your Kindle Fire, your computer, and a smartphone.

Modifying Your Account Settings

When you have your e-mail account set up, you can modify the default settings to automatically check mail less frequently or append a text signature to your outgoing messages.

1. Swipe down from the status bar to open Settings.

2. Tap More.

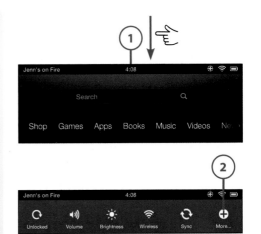

3. Tap Applications.

4. Tap E-mail, Contacts, Calendars.

5. Tap an e-mail account to modify its account settings.

6. Turn syncing of e-mail, the calendar, or contacts on or off.

7. Tap to change the frequency with which your Kindle Fire checks for e-mail.

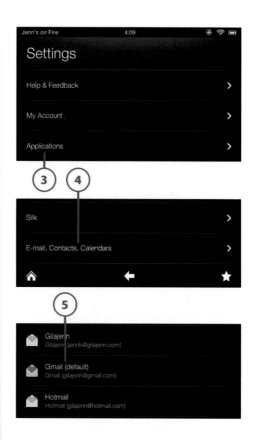

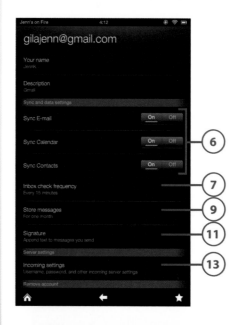

8. Choose a new setting for Inbox Check Frequency.

9. Tap to change how long your Kindle Fire stores old e-mail messages.

10. Select a new duration for storing messages.

11. Tap to create a signature line that's automatically appended to every message you send from this e-mail account.

12. Type a signature line and then tap OK. This is usually your name and title or a message stating that you're typing on your Kindle Fire (which can serve as a warning to recipients that you're not fully responsible for typos).

13. Tap to change the server settings. This opens the account setup screen so that you can change the password or server information for your account.

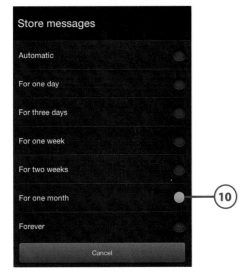

>>Go Further

CHANGING E-MAIL GENERAL SETTINGS

Aside from the settings specific to each account, you can modify the general settings for the E-mail app. To do this, choose E-mail General Settings from the E-mail, Contacts, Calendars page. From the General Settings page, you can change the text size of messages, instruct the Kindle Fire to show or hide images embedded in the messages you receive, and decide whether to quote the original message when you reply to an e-mail.

You can also tell the Kindle Fire to automatically download attachments. I recommend leaving this option set to the default, which is not to automatically download attachments. This protects you against downloading a virus and keeps you in control of how your storage is used on your Kindle Fire. You can always manually download the attachments you want to keep on your device.

Removing an Account

If you change e-mail providers or no longer want your Kindle Fire to check an account for e-mail, you can remove it from your Kindle Fire.

1. From the E-mail, Contacts, Calendars page, type the account you want to remove.

2. Scroll to the bottom of the account settings screen.

3. Tap Remove Account.

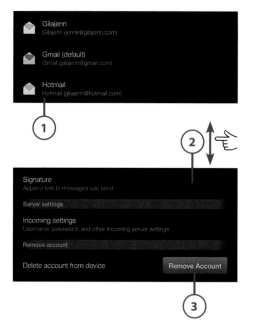

4. Tap OK to confirm the deletion of the account.

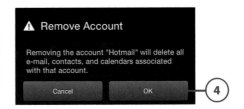

Deleting an Account Deletes Your Data

When you remove an account from your Kindle Fire, all the e-mail, contacts, and calendars associated with that account are deleted. If you remove a POP3 account and did not have your messages saved on the server, those messages are gone forever.

Managing Your E-mail Inbox

The E-mail app is preinstalled in the Apps library on your Kindle fire. It is also automatically added to your Favorites drawer. When you open it the first time, the app also appears on your home screen Carousel.

Your inbox is where you can view all the e-mail messages you have received. Without opening a mail message, you can see who sent the mail, the subject of the e-mail, and a brief snippet of the message. You can also flag your mail, sort it, and delete messages you aren't interested in.

Choosing an Inbox

Your inbox can display e-mail messages from a single account or in a combined account view that shows all messages from all accounts.

1. From your inbox, tap an account name.

2. Select a different account to view the inbox for that account.

3. Select Combined Inbox to view the inbox for all the accounts at once.

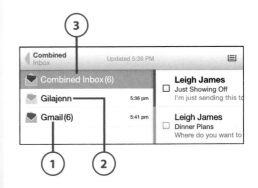

Determining the Source of a Message

Each e-mail account is color-coded when you add it to your Kindle Fire. As you scroll through your combined inbox, the color of the bar to the left of the message identifies which account it came from.

Choosing a Folder

Most e-mail providers enable you to create folders so that you can organize e-mail that you want to keep. You can choose which folder is displayed when viewing an account's inbox.

1. From your account inbox, tap the Inbox button to open the account menu.

2. Tap Show Folders.

3. Select a folder to display the messages in that folder.

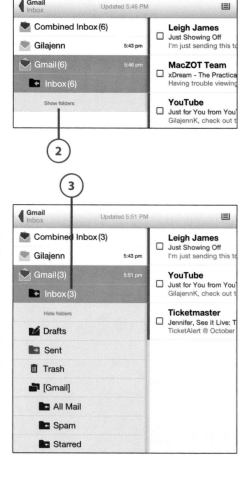

It's Not All Good

Creating Folders

You can use folders on your Kindle Fire, but you can't create them on the device. To create folders for your e-mail account, you have to use an e-mail program on your computer or in your web browser. Those folders are then synced with your Kindle Fire the next time it checks your e-mail.

Searching E-mail

You can search your e-mail messages.

1. Tap the Search icon.

2. Enter the text you want to search for.

3. Tap the part of the message you want to search.

4. Tap a message from your search results to open the message. You can search the subject, the To field, and the From field for all message types. You can search the entire message for IMAP and POP3 accounts.

5. Tap the back arrow to exit the search.

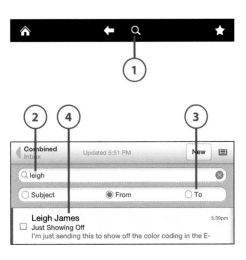

You Can't Search the Text of a Message

The search function in e-mail is very limited. You cannot search the text of a message unless the e-mail account type supports it. If you use the combined inbox and one of the accounts doesn't support searching the text of a message, that type of search is unavailable for all messages in the combined inbox. IMAP supports full message search, but Gmail does not.

Synchronizing E-mail and Loading More Messages

Your Kindle Fire automatically checks for mail with the frequency you selected in the account settings. You can manually synchronize at any time to check for new messages between update intervals. The Kindle Fire downloads 25 messages at a time, but you can request more.

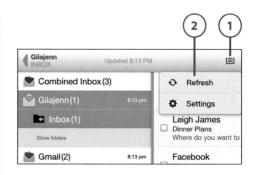

1. From your inbox, tap the menu icon.

2. Tap Refresh.

3. To load additional messages, scroll to the bottom of your inbox.

4. Tap Load More Messages.

Requesting Additional Messages

The Load More Messages option appears only on POP3 and IMAP accounts.

Selecting and Managing Multiple Messages

You can select one or more messages in your inbox and then choose to delete them, move them to another folder, or mark them as read or unread.

1. Tap the check box next to the messages you want to select.

2. Tap Delete to delete the messages.

3. Tap Move to move the messages to another folder.

4. Choose a folder to move the messages into.

5. Tap Mark to open the Mark menu.

6. Mark the messages as read or unread. This menu item is a toggle, based on whether the selected messages are currently read or unread.

7. Tap Star to flag a message as important. Flagged messages appear with a star under the date and time received.

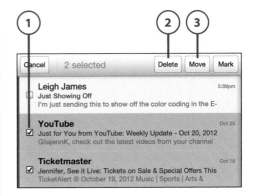

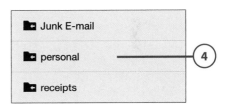

Reading E-mail

Having e-mail on your Kindle Fire is a great convenience. Not only is it nice to browse your mail while you relax on the couch, but it's also easy to triage your e-mail from the Kindle Fire. By that, I mean that you can quickly peruse your inbox and delete junk mail or other mail you're not interested in, move mail to another folder, mark important mail for follow-up later, and so forth. Then when you sit down at your computer, you know exactly which messages are worth your attention.

Reading a Message

While reading a message, you can view address details, delete the message, move it to another folder, or flag it with a star.

1. Tap a message in your inbox to open it.

2. Tap Details/Hide Details to display or hide the recipients of the message, including the Cc: list.

3. Tap Newer to read the next message up in your inbox.

4. Tap Older to read the next-oldest message in your inbox.

5. Tap Delete to delete the message.

6. Tap Respond to reply to the message.

7. Tap Reply to reply to the sender.

8. Tap Reply All to reply to the sender and everyone on the To: or Cc: list.

9. Tap Forward to forward the message and any attachments to a new recipient.

10. Tap New to compose a new message.

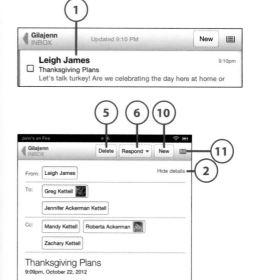

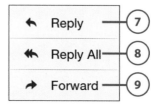

11. Tap the menu button for more options.

12. Tap Move to move the message into another folder.

13. Tap Star to flag the message as important.

14. Tap Mark Unread to mark the message as unread in your inbox.

15. Tap Settings to go to the E-mail, Contacts, Calendars page to change either account settings or general settings for your e-mail.

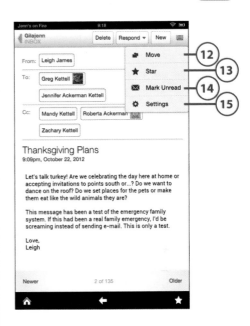

Viewing Attachments

Your Kindle Fire comes with apps that can view many file types, including images, videos in MP4 format, PDF files, and Microsoft Office documents. If you receive attachments in these formats, you can download and access them on your Kindle Fire.

1. Tap a mail message containing an attachment. A paperclip appears on messages with attachments in the inbox.

2. Tap the attachment. The file downloads, and the icon changes to show the format of the file.

3. Tap and hold the attachment to open the attachment menu.

4. Tap Open to open the attachment in an appropriate app.

5. Tap Save to save the attachment onto your Kindle Fire.

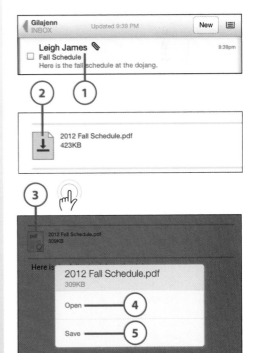

Opening Saved Attachments

When you save an attachment, your Kindle Fire automatically puts the file in the appropriate library. PDFs are stored in your Docs library, for example.

Composing a New E-mail Message

You can compose a new e-mail either while viewing your inbox or while viewing a message.

1. Tap the New icon.

2. Enter the e-mail address of the recipient of your message. Separate multiple e-mail addresses with a comma.

3. Tap the plus (+) sign to select a contact from your Contacts app. For more information on the Contacts app, see Chapter 11, "Managing Your Personal Documents and Data."

4. Tap Options.

5. Enter one or more e-mail addresses in the Cc: field if you want additional people copied on your message.

6. Enter one or more e-mail addresses in the Bcc: field if you want to copy additional people on your message without the other recipients seeing their address(es).

7. Tap your e-mail address in the From: field if you want to change which account sends the message.

8. Enter a subject for your message.

9. Enter the text of the message.

10. Tap Attach to attach a file to your message.

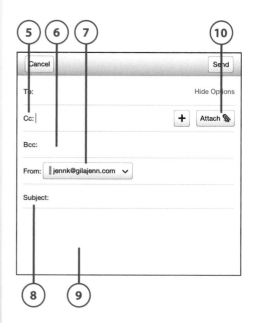

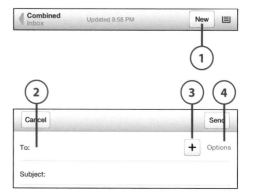

11. Choose an app to use for browsing to the file you want to attach.

12. Select the file you want to attach using the app you selected.

13. Tap the X to remove an attached file.

14. Tap Send to send your message.

15. Tap Cancel if you decide not to send your message right away.

16. Tap Save Draft if you want to save the message to edit and send later.

17. Tap Delete Draft to cancel and delete the message.

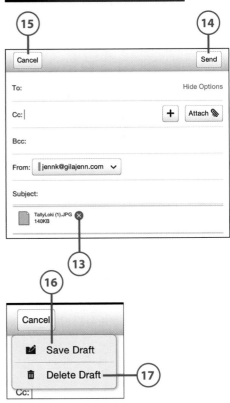

Schedule events

Manage your contacts

Read and edit your personal documents

Quick access to contacts and your calendar

In this chapter, you learn how to maintain the documents and contact information that convert your Kindle Fire from a content viewer into a personal management tool. Topics include the following:

→ Managing personal documents
→ Using the contacts app

Managing Your Personal Documents and Data

Life is messy. You accumulate all manner of bits and pieces of information, phone numbers, and appointments just going about your day. You learned in earlier chapters how to use your Kindle Fire to view content and access some apps to help you connect with friends and manage your e-mail. Until you understand how to use your Kindle Fire to organize those other aspects of your life, though, it won't be a truly reliable companion.

The Kindle Fire provides tools to organize and retrieve your personal documents, including spreadsheets and Word .doc and .docx files. The Contacts app keeps track of all the people in your life and integrates with the E-mail app to make reaching them easy.

Managing Personal Documents

In Chapter 2, "Loading Your Kindle Fire," you learned how to use your Cloud Drive and how to sideload to get personal documents onto your Kindle Fire. In Chapter 3, "Using Amazon's Manage Your Kindle

Page," you learned how to e-mail personal documents to your Kindle Fire. No matter which of these techniques you use to transfer documents onto your device, when your documents are in your library, you can easily access them.

Viewing PDF Documents

Your experience in reading personal documents differs depending on what type of file the document is. The Kindle Fire can read PDFs with the built-in Adobe PDF reader.

1. From the Home screen, tap Docs.

2. The format of files in your Docs library is evident from the color-coding and the format name on the icon. Tap a PDF document.

3. Double-tap to zoom in on the page.

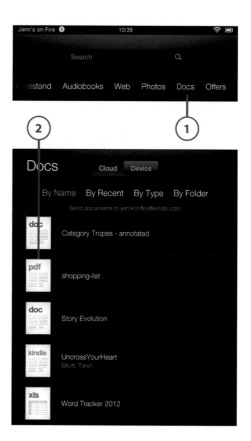

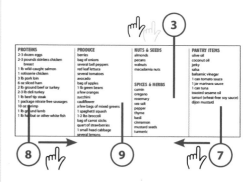

4. Reverse-pinch to enlarge a particular area.

5. Pinch to zoom out.

6. Tap and slide to move around the page.

7. Tap the right side of the page or swipe from right to left to advance one page.

8. Tap the left side of the page or swipe from left to right to go back one page.

9. Tap the middle of the page to display the PDF controls.

10. Slide the location bar to quickly move to another page in the document.

11. Tap the Back button to return to your Docs library.

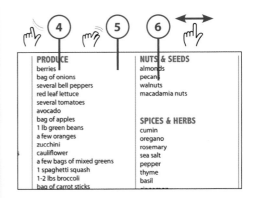

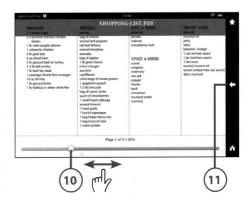

Rotating Landscape-Formatted PDFs

PDF documents open full-screen, depending on the orientation of your Kindle Fire and the document layout. Rotate your Kindle Fire to landscape orientation for better viewing of landscape-layout documents.

Viewing Word Documents

Personal documents in .txt, .doc, .docx, and .rtf formats open in OfficeSuite. This preinstalled app enables you to view your files and get a word count, but it does not allow you to edit the files.

1. In your Docs library, tap a DOC-formatted file.

2. Double-tap the page to quickly zoom in or out.

3. Scroll down to continue reading the document. Word processing documents are not paginated in the same way as PDFs, so your file will scroll as one long page.

4. Tap Word Count to see how many words, characters, and paragraphs are in the document.

5. Tap OK to return to the document.

6. Tap Find to search the document.

7. Enter your search criteria.

8. Tap Next to see the next occurrence of your search term.

9. Tap Previous to see the previous occurrence of your search term.

10. Tap Done to exit the search.

11. Tap the menu icon to access the View options.

12. Tap View to navigate through your document.

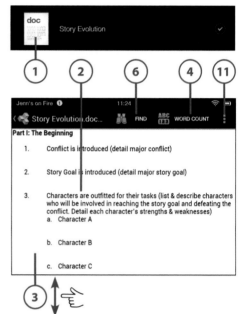

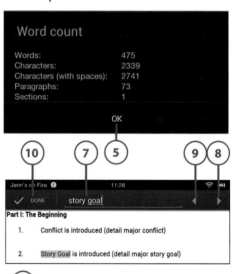

13. Tap Go to Top to jump to the top of the document.

14. Tap Go to Bottom to jump to the bottom of the document.

Viewing Spreadsheets

OfficeSuite also enables you to view spreadsheets. Again, you can look at the file and open charts, but you cannot edit the spreadsheet.

1. From the Docs library, tap to open an .xls- or .xlsx-formatted spreadsheet.

2. Double-tap the page to quickly zoom in or out. Use the same gestures to navigate through the spreadsheet as you would a document.

3. Tap Sheets to see a list of all the sheets in the worksheet.

4. Choose a sheet. (Not all spreadsheets have multiple worksheets.)

5. Tap Charts to see any charts that are embedded in the spreadsheet.

6. Tap the menu button to access additional options.

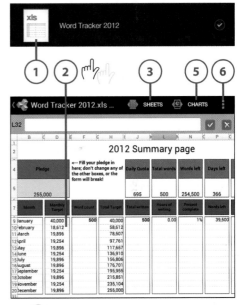

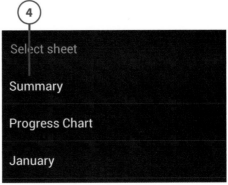

7. Tap Go To to find a specific cell.

8. Enter the cell coordinates.

9. Tap Go.

Can't Edit Spreadsheets

When you navigate through the cells of a spreadsheet, you can see the formulas that were used to calculate each cell, but you cannot edit them.

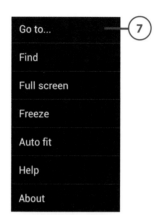

Go to... 7

Find

Full screen

Freeze

Auto fit

Help

About

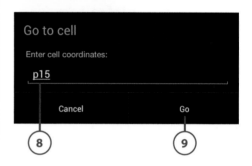

Go to cell

Enter cell coordinates:

p15

Cancel   Go

8   9

>>>Go Further

EDITING WORD DOCUMENTS AND SPREADSHEETS

If you want to edit documents and spreadsheets on your Kindle Fire, you can purchase one of several Office suites available in the Appstore. OfficeSuite Pro extends the capabilities of the preinstalled OfficeSuite to allow you to edit files. You might want to compare the features in OfficeSuite Pro with those of Documents to Go or Quickoffice Pro. Each of these apps costs $14.99, but occasionally you can find one listed as the Free App of the Day in the Appstore.

Using the Contacts App

Your Kindle Fire's Contacts app makes it easy to maintain a list of contacts for e-mail messages or for reference. You can easily import contacts from another source into your Kindle Fire. If you make changes to your contacts on the Kindle Fire and want to apply those changes to your contact list in another e-mail application, you can export your Kindle Fire contacts so that you can use them elsewhere.

Viewing Contacts

You can view your contacts from the Contacts app.

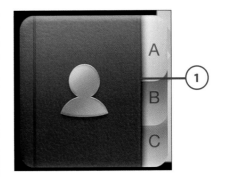

1. Open the Contacts app. You can access it from the Apps library, your Carousel, or the Quick Links.

2. Tap All to view all your contacts.

3. Tap Favorites to view contacts that you've marked as your favorites.

4. Tap and hold the scrollbar to quickly scroll through the alphabet.

5. Tap a contact to view contact details.

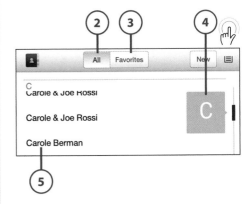

Favorite Contacts

You can add a contact to your favorites list by viewing the entry's contact details and then tapping the star.

Adding a Contact

When you meet someone new, add that person's contact information to the Contacts app.

1. Tap the New button.

2. Select which account you want to use to synchronize your contacts. If you did not already set up your accounts in Chapter 10, "Reading and Sending E-mail," tap Add New Account to link your Kindle Fire with your webmail account.

3. Enter the name information for your contact.

4. Enter the phone number.

5. Select the type of phone number you entered.

6. Enter the e-mail address and select the type.

7. Enter the address and select the type.

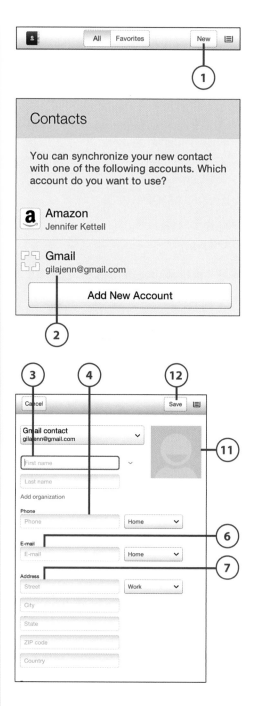

8. Enter your contact's birthday.

9. Tap Add Another Field to enter more information.

10. Choose the type of information you want to add to the contact record.

11. Tap the picture icon to add a picture of the contact. The picture must already be on your Kindle Fire.

12. Tap Save.

Synchronizing Contacts

You can synchronize your contacts with only one account. If you use Gmail or another webmail service to manage your contacts and calendars on your other devices, choose the same account here so that your data stays in sync.

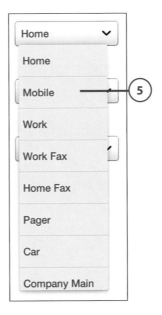

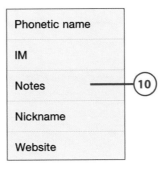

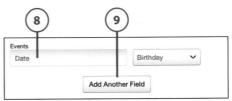

Editing a Contact

You can edit existing contacts.

1. On the contact details screen, tap Edit.
2. Edit the information as necessary and tap Save.

Changing Contact Sort Order and Name Display

By default, contacts are sorted by first name, which can make it difficult to easily locate the contact you seek. You can change the sort order of your contacts and how names are displayed.

1. From your contact list, tap the menu icon and then tap Settings.
2. Tap Contacts General Settings.

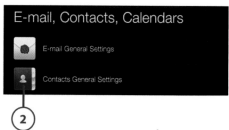

3. Tap Sort Order of Contact Name.

4. Tap Last, First to sort your con-
    tacts list by last name.

5. Tap Display Order of Contact
    Name, and then choose how you
    want names to be displayed in
    the contacts list.

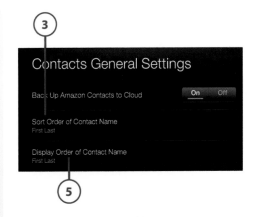

Contacts General Settings

Back Up Amazon Contacts to Cloud   On   Off

Sort Order of Contact Name
First Last

Display Order of Contact Name
First Last

Sort Order of Contact Name

First Last

Last, First

Cancel

Use tabs to browse
multiple sites

Bookmark your
favorite sites

Browse
websites

See what
sites other
Kindle Fire
users are
viewing
most

In this chapter, you learn how to use Silk, the web browser that's included with your Kindle Fire. Topics include the following:

→ Browsing the web
→ Working with tabs
→ Using bookmarks and history
→ Downloading files
→ Configuring Silk settings

Browsing the Web with Silk

Your Kindle Fire includes a web browser called Silk. Silk is a full-featured browser with support for most of today's modern web standards.

You'll likely find that browsing on a tablet device is a mixed bag. Some sites look and work great; others might not work as well. Tapping a specific link can be difficult when hyperlinks on a page appear too close to each other. (You can solve that problem by zooming in on the page.) Even with these drawbacks, though, having the ability to browse the Internet easily from your favorite chair is a great convenience.

Browsing the Web

Silk works similarly to the web browser that you use on your computer. One major difference is that, instead of using a mouse, you use touch to navigate with Silk.

In this section, you learn the basics of using Silk. In the sections that follow, I explain additional features, such as using favorites and tabs, to help you get the most out of Silk.

Using the Starter Page

When you first open Silk, the Starter page opens. The Starter page suggests websites based on three different criteria.

1. From the Home screen, tap Web to launch Silk. Silk is also added to your Favorites drawer by default.

2. Swipe through Most Visited to see the sites you visit most frequently. The pages that appear in this area change as you use Silk.

3. Swipe through Trending Now to see sites visited by other Silk users, as tracked by Amazon from users' page views.

4. Swipe through Selected Sites to see sites of general interest, such as shopping, entertainment, and information sites.

5. Tap a site to open the page.

Returning to the Starter Page

You can return to the Starter page from any other site by tapping the menu icon at the bottom of the page and then tapping Starter Page.

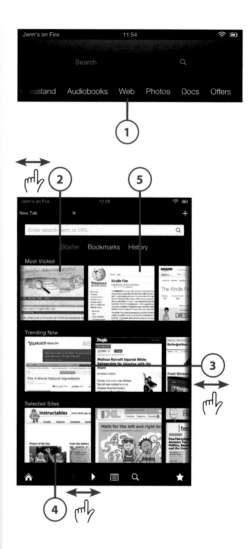

It's Not All Good

Opting Out of Trending Now

Trending Now suggestions appear on the Starter page in Silk and below the carousel on the Home page. These pages are compiled by Amazon's tracking of pages viewed by Kindle Fire users. If the privacy implications of this bother you, there is a way to opt out. If you select Optional Encryption in the Silk Settings, Amazon no longer caches your browser history, thus disabling the Trending Now feature. The downside is that pages might load slower. I explain how to access Silk Settings later in this chapter.

Browsing to a Website

You can enter a URL and browse directly to a website.

1. In the browser, tap inside the address bar.

2. Enter a URL. As you type, Silk attempts to home in on the URL you seek.

3. Tap one of the suggested entries when your destination appears. You can also type a complete URL and tap the Go button on the keyboard.

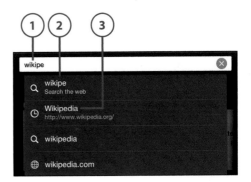

Navigating a Page

Web pages open full screen. You can navigate the page using zoom and pan techniques.

1. Browse to a URL.

2. Double-tap an area to zoom in.

3. Drag to move around the page.

4. Reverse-pinch to zoom in on the page.

5. Pinch to zoom out on the page.

6. Tap a link to follow the link.

7. Double-tap to zoom back to full-page view.

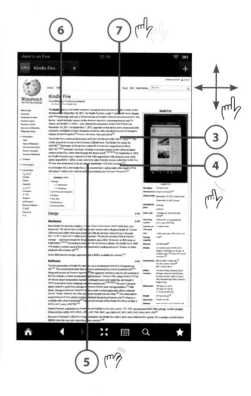

It's Not All Good

No Support for Flash

Some web pages cannot be viewed properly in Silk because they use Flash, which is a method of adding animation and interactivity to websites. The Kindle Fire HD does not support Flash. If you've upgraded from a first-generation Kindle Fire, the loss of this feature might be disappointing, but it's not Amazon's fault. Adobe, the creator of Flash, has decided to no longer support Flash on any tablet or smartphone devices.

Sharing Pages on Facebook

When you find a page that you want to share with your Facebook friends, you can do it easily.

1. From the page that you want to share, tap the menu icon.

2. Tap Share Page.

3. Tap Facebook.

4. Enter a comment about the page.

5. Tap Share to post the page and your comment on your Wall.

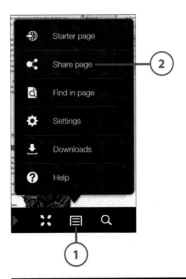

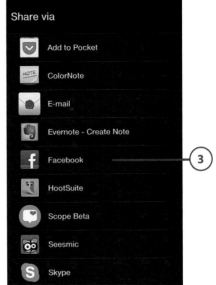

Sharing Pages with E-mail

You can also share a page by sending a link through e-mail.

1. From the Share Via menu, tap E-mail.

2. Enter one or more e-mail addresses.

3. Add a message, if you want.

4. Tap Send to send from your default e-mail account.

Sharing with Other Apps

Many other apps have the capability to share links from Silk. Installed apps with this feature also appear in the Share Via menu.

Copying a Link to the Current Page

You can copy a link to the current page so that you can paste it into a document.

1. Scroll to the top of the page so that the URL is visible.

2. Tap and hold the URL in the address bar.

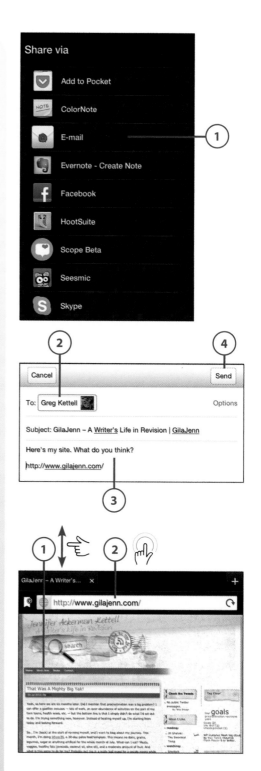

3. Tap Copy to copy the URL so that you can paste it elsewhere. You can paste the URL on another page within Silk or even in another app.

Pasting URLs

To paste a URL, tap and hold, and then tap Paste. You can paste into the address bar in Silk, the subject or text of an e-mail message, or in many other apps.

Copying a Hyperlink on a Page

You can also copy a hyperlink that appears on a page.

1. Tap and hold a hyperlink.
2. Tap Copy Link URL.

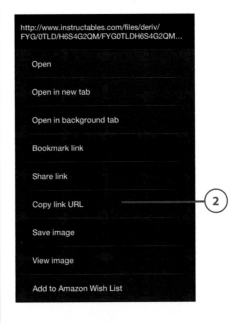

Saving Images

If you tap and hold an image on a web page, you have the option to save the image in your Photos library.

Searching in the Current Page

You can search for text within the current page.

1. While viewing the page, tap the menu icon.

2. Tap Find in Page.

3. Enter your search term. As you type, search results are highlighted on the page.

4. Tap Done to close the keyboard so that you can see more of the page.

5. Tap the Next Result icon to highlight the next result.

6. Tap the Previous Result icon to highlight the previous result.

7. Tap Done to stop searching.

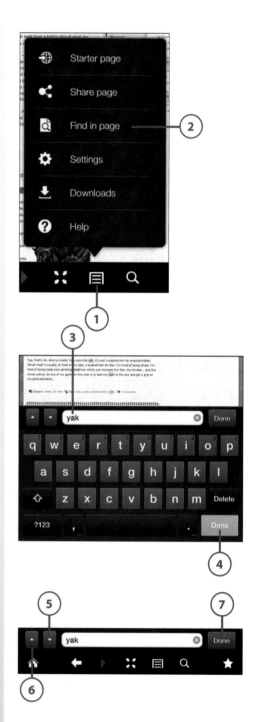

Searching the Web

Whenever you begin typing in the address bar, Silk offers the option to search for the term you enter.

1. Scroll to the top of the page so that the address bar is visible, and tap the address bar.

2. Enter your search term. The URL that was in the address bar is replaced with what you type.

3. Tap Go (on the keyboard) or tap a search suggestion to search using your configured search engine.

Your Search Engine

The default search engine is Bing, but you can change it in Silk's settings, if you want. I show you how later in this chapter.

Working with Tabs

After you tap a link on a website, you can always tap the Back button to return to the previous page, but using tabs is much more convenient. Tabs enable you to have more than one web page open at the same time. You can flip between pages by tapping the tab that contains the page you want to view.

Because each tab is using resources on your Kindle Fire, Silk limits you to a total of 10 open tabs at a time.

Opening Links in a New Tab

When you tap a link, the new page opens in the same tab by default. However, you can choose to open a link in a new tab so that you can have both the original page and the new page open at the same time. You can also open a new tab in the background so that you can view it when you're done with the current page.

1. Tap and hold a link that you want to follow. Zoom in on the page, if necessary, to accurately tap the link.

2. Tap Open in New Tab to open the page in a new tab and immediately make it the active tab.

3. Tap Open in Background Tab to open the page in a new tab but remain on the current tab as the active tab.

Navigating Tabs

You can add a new tab so that you can browse to a new page while leaving the current page open in a different tab. You can then close a single tab or multiple tabs.

1. Tap the Add Tab icon to add a new tab.

2. Tap the Close icon to close a tab.

3. If you have too many tabs open to see at once, swipe to locate a desired tab.

4. Tap and hold a tab to close multiple tabs.

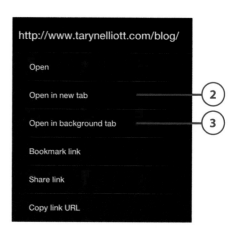

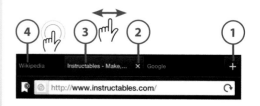

5. Tap Close Other Tabs to close all tabs except for the active tab.

6. Tap Close All Tabs to close all the tabs and return to the Starter page.

Always One Tab

Even if you tap Close All Tabs, one tab remains open and displays the Starter page. If you tap the Close icon on this tab, Silk closes and returns you to the Home screen.

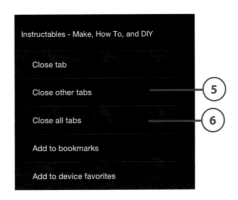

Using Bookmarks and History

Bookmarks are an easy way to return to a page at any time. Bookmarks aren't just convenient for saving your favorite sites. You can also use them to temporarily save links to websites while you are researching a particular topic. For example, you can save bookmarks to product reviews so that you can easily refer back to them when deciding which item to purchase.

Bookmarking the Current Page

You can bookmark any page that you are currently viewing.

1. Scroll to the top of the page you want to bookmark.

2. Tap the Add Bookmark button to the left of the address bar.

3. Edit the name of the bookmark (or you can just go with the default).

4. Tap OK to save the bookmark.

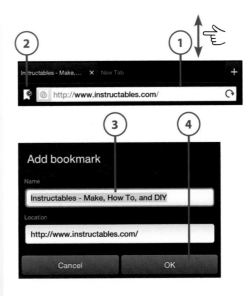

Bookmarking a Hyperlink

You can bookmark a hyperlink without following the link.

1. Tap and hold the hyperlink that you want to bookmark.

2. Tap Bookmark Link.

3. Enter a name for the bookmark.

4. Edit the URL, if desired. You can shorten a link to a specific page on a site to the main URL for the site, for example.

5. Tap OK to save your bookmark.

Viewing and Following Bookmarks

You can view all your bookmarks on one page and then tap to follow one.

1. On the Starter page, tap Bookmarks.

2. Tap a bookmark to go to that page.

3. Tap the menu button to change the view of the bookmarks.

4. Tap List View to view the bookmarks in a list. Tap Grid View to return to the default view.

5. Tap Add Bookmark to create a new bookmark without first navigating to the URL.

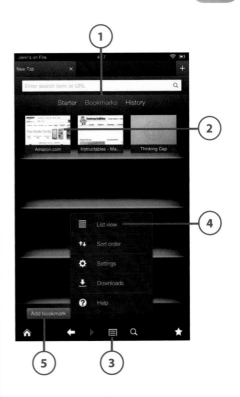

Editing a Bookmark

You can edit the name or location of a bookmark.

1. From the Bookmarks screen, tap and hold the bookmark you want to edit.

2. Tap Edit Bookmark.

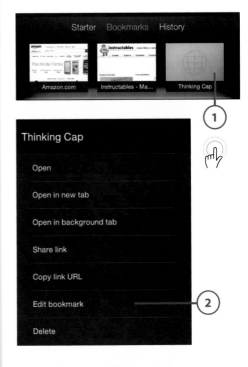

3. Make the desired changes to your bookmark.

4. Tap OK to save the bookmark.

Deleting a Bookmark

The process to delete a bookmark is much the same. Tap and hold the bookmark you want to delete, and then tap Delete from the menu.

Viewing History

As you browse the Web, Silk keeps a record of where you've been. You can view your browsing history for the last seven days so that you can return to a page you've previously visited.

1. From the Starter or Bookmarks page, tap History.

2. Tap a section to expand or collapse the history by that date.

3. Tap an entry to browse to that page.

4. Tap and hold an entry to bring up the options to open the page in a new tab, share the link, copy the link URL, or add a bookmark.

5. Tap the X to delete that page from your history.

6. Tap Clear All to delete the entire history.

Downloading Files

You can download files using Silk. Files that are downloaded are available on the Downloads screen. You can access the Downloads screen by tapping the menu icon while browsing and then tapping Downloads.

Although it doesn't make sense to download some types of files (executable files that install software on a computer, for example), you might want to download eBook files, PDF files, .doc or .docx files (Microsoft Word), pictures, or MP4 videos.

It's Not All Good

Be Cautious of Downloading Files

The Internet isn't always a safe place. Before you download a file, make sure you trust the source of the file. Numerous Android viruses can infect your Kindle Fire, and a common source of Android viruses is infected apps and files. You can keep yourself safe by downloading files from only known, reputable websites. For example, if you're downloading a PDF manual of your new TV set from the manufacturer's website, you'll be fine. If you locate what appears to be a PDF manual from a different website, you're better off getting it from the manufacturer's site.

When you download a file, your Kindle Fire uses the file's extension (the letters after the period in the filename) to determine which one of your apps can handle opening the file. If you have more than one app installed that can open the file, you're prompted to select an app to use. You can also choose an app as the default app for that particular file type.

Starting and Monitoring Downloads

After starting a download, you can see a list of your downloads and monitor it easily.

1. Tap a downloadable link to start the download.

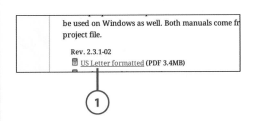

2. To monitor your download, tap the menu icon.

3. Tap Downloads.

4. Tap a download that has completed.

Identifying File Types

If the Kindle Fire can identify which app supports the downloaded file, it opens immediately. Otherwise, you're prompted to choose an application to open the downloaded file.

Sharing Downloaded Files

You can share downloaded files as e-mail attachments, via Skype, and with other apps, such as Evernote, that utilize this feature.

1. From the Downloads screen, tap the check box to select the file or files you want to share.

2. Tap the Share button.

3. Tap the app you want to use to share the downloaded file, such as E-mail.

4. Enter the name of the person you want to send the downloaded file to.

5. Enter a subject for the message.

6. Enter additional text to the message, if necessary.

7. Tap Send to send the e-mail from your default account.

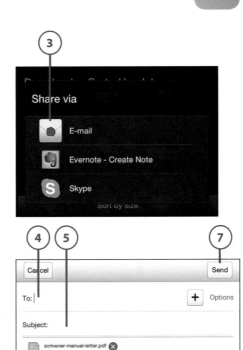

Deleting Downloaded Files

You can delete downloaded files to free up space on your Kindle Fire.

1. From the Downloads screen, tap the check box to select the file or files you want to delete.

2. Tap the Trash button.

Be Sure Before Deleting Downloaded Files

No confirmation or warning appears before you delete a downloaded file, so be certain you're deleting the correct file before you tap the Trash button.

Configuring Silk Settings

Several settings in Silk help you get the most out of your Kindle Fire. I don't cover all the settings here, but here are a couple that are useful.

All of Silk's settings are on the Settings screen. To access the Settings screen, tap the menu icon while browsing and then tap the Settings icon. The Silk Settings are grouped into General, Saved Data, and Advanced settings to help you navigate the lengthy menu.

Setting Your Search Engine

Silk uses Bing as the default search engine. If you have a different favorite, you can select it.

1. From the Silk Settings, tap Search Engine.

2. Select a search engine. Choose from Bing, Yahoo!, or Google.

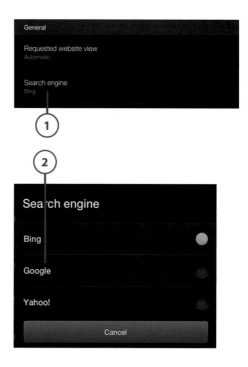

Enable Location

Some sites request access to your location so that they can tag your messages with location data or show you ads specific to your region. You can deny sites access to this data.

1. From the Silk Settings, tap Enable Location to clear the check box and disable this feature.

2. Tap the check box again if you change your mind and want to allow Silk to share location data.

A blue background
lets you see at a
glance that your
child is in FreeTime

Search is limited
to the child's
content

Each child has a
separate Carousel
and content

Locate content by
character or theme
for nonreaders

In this chapter, you learn how to configure parental controls and Kindle FreeTime to create a safe environment for your child to enjoy the Kindle Fire. Topics include these:

→ Setting up Kindle FreeTime
→ Teaching your kids how to use Kindle FreeTime
→ Parental controls for older children

13

Giving Your Kids a Kindle Fire

The Kindle Fire is perfect for kids. The device itself is solid, with a display that's 30 times harder than plastic, so accidental drops and bangs aren't likely to do major damage.

The Kindle Fire offers two types of parental controls. Kindle FreeTime is a brand new service for families with young children. FreeTime provides a child-friendly customized interface and allows parents to customize the specific books, music, videos, and apps children can view. The standard parental controls are for older children who are mature enough for the regular Kindle Fire interface and who do not require time restrictions but aren't yet ready to be given free rein over the content they use.

Setting Up Kindle FreeTime

Kindle FreeTime is a preinstalled app that turns your Kindle Fire into a kid-friendly device. FreeTime blocks access to Silk and the Amazon Store. It disables GameCircle and sharing to the Kindle Community,

Facebook, and Twitter. In-app purchases require a password, which prevents your child from making unexpected purchases on your credit card.

You can create a separate profile for each child and give each profile access to specific content. You can set limits on how much screen time each child is allowed on the Kindle Fire. FreeTime also provides a kid-friendly interface for your children, with a blue background and larger font size for text, and a search feature for nonreaders.

FreeTime requires setup before you put the Kindle Fire into your young child's hands.

Accessing Kindle FreeTime

The parent account provides password-protected access to the Kindle FreeTime settings.

1. From the Apps library, tap Kindle FreeTime.

2. The intro screen explains the basic steps to get started. Tap Next.

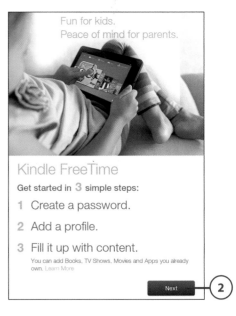

Fun for kids.
Peace of mind for parents.

Kindle FreeTime

Get started in 3 simple steps:

1 Create a password.

2 Add a profile.

3 Fill it up with content.
You can add Books, TV Shows, Movies and Apps you already own. Learn More

Next

3. Enter your parental controls password. If you have not yet set a password for parental controls, you are prompted to create one.

4. Tap OK.

Setting Up Child Profiles

Each child in your family can have an individual profile on Kindle FreeTime.

1. After you enter your parental controls password, you're immediately prompted to create a child profile. Enter your child's name.

2. Select your child's gender.

3. Tap to enter your child's date of birth.

4. Use the sliders to set your child's birthdate.

5. Tap Set.

6. Tap to set a photo for the profile.

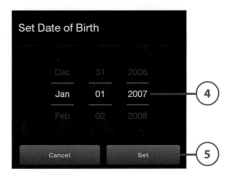

7. Tap an avatar your child can use to identify the profile.

8. Tap Next if you want to set up FreeTime for one child.

9. Tap Add Another Child to set up additional profiles, and then tap Next when you are finished entering profiles. You can create up to six profiles on your Kindle Fire.

Completing Profile Setup

After you set up child profiles, the Kindle FreeTime app opens to the start page whenever you open the app in the future. If you need to change a profile or add another child, tap Manage Child Profiles on the start page.

Manage Content on FreeTime

After creating a profile for each child, you can customize the settings so your children each have access to the content you think is appropriate.

Shop First, Add Content Later

Kindle FreeTime does not have access to the Amazon Store, so purchase content for your children before opening FreeTime to manage content. Of course, you can always add more content to your child's profile when you make future purchases.

1. From the Kindle FreeTime start page, tap Manage Content.

2. Enter your parental controls password.

3. Tap OK.

4. Tap Add Titles to [Your Child's] Library.

5. Tap Books, Videos, or Apps to select a type of content.

6. Tap the box to the right of each title you want to add to the profile.

7. Tap Save.

8. Tap the Back button to return to the FreeTime start page.

Adding Videos to FreeTime

You must purchase videos for use with FreeTime. You cannot add video rentals or content from Prime Instant Video to child profiles.

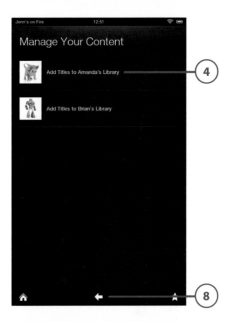

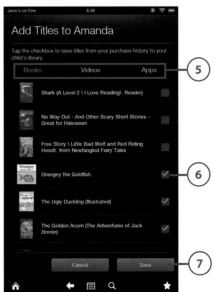

Setting Daily Time Limits

You can set time limits for how long your child can use the Kindle Fire. Alternatively, you can define different limits for each type of content, such as allowing unlimited reading time but only one hour for apps.

1. From the FreeTime start page, tap Daily Time Limits.

2. Enter your parental controls password.

3. Tap OK.

4. Tap a child's profile.

5. Tap On. The screen expands to open the time limit controls.

6. Use the slider to set a total daily usage limit for the Kindle Fire.

7. Tap Content Activity Time to set limits based on type of content.

8. Use the slider to set a time limit for Reading Books.

9. Use the slider to set a time limit for Watching Videos. The slider adjusts in 15-minute increments.

10. Use the slider to set a time limit for Using Apps. This setting does not distinguish between educational apps and games.

11. Tap the Back button.

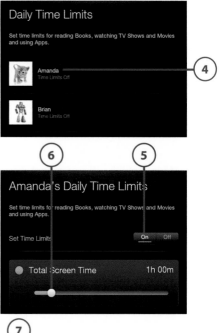

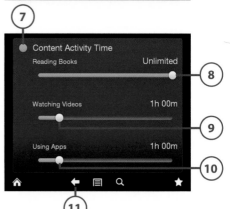

12. Tap another profile to set time limits or tap the Back button to return to the start page.

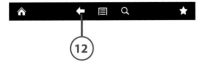

SHOULD I SET A LIMIT ON READING BOOKS?

Most parents want to encourage their children to read, so the default setting for Reading Books on FreeTime is Unlimited. If your child has vision problems, however, you might want to limit overall screen time, to foster time away from the screen. Also, studies have shown that backlit screen time just before bed can affect a child's sleep, so you might want to encourage reading traditional paper books (or E Ink–based devices such as Kindle Paperwhite) at bedtime.

Changing the Parental Controls Password

You can change your parental controls password.

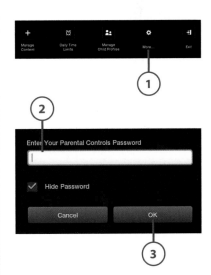

1. From the FreeTime start page, tap More.

2. Enter your current parental controls password.

3. Tap OK.

4. Tap Change Parental Controls Password.

5. Enter your current password.

6. Type a new password.

7. Reenter the new password.

8. Tap Finish.

It's Not All Good

Remember Your Password

If you forget your parental controls password, you need to restore your Kindle Fire to factory settings. This wipes out all your Amazon account information, downloaded content, and personal documents, photos, and videos.

If you need to restore your Kindle Fire to factory settings, swipe down from the status bar to open Settings and then tap More. Tap Device and then tap Reset to Factory Defaults. Be sure you've first backed up any personal content you want to keep to your Cloud Drive or computer.

Teaching Your Kids How to Use Kindle FreeTime

After setting up FreeTime, tap a child's profile from the start page to enter that child's FreeTime account. The Kindle Fire interface changes to a controlled, kid-friendly environment. The content that you have added to the child's profile is available in the appropriate Books, Videos, and Apps categories. Content also appears on the Carousel.

It's Not All Good

Preinstalled Content on FreeTime

In addition to the content you put on your child's profile, Amazon has made some of its own selections. FreeTime comes with several books and apps preinstalled. Some parents might not appreciate Amazon choosing content for their children. Unfortunately, you need to individually download each book or app within the child's account before you can choose to remove it from the device (tap and hold the item, and then choose Remove from Device). If you object to any of the preinstalled content, you should download and remove it before giving the Kindle Fire to your child.

Using the FreeTime Interface

Although children seem to inherently know how to operate electronic devices, and the FreeTime interface is very intuitive, here are some tips for you to help your child get started.

1. Swipe along the Carousel to browse new or recently used books, apps, and videos.

2. Tap Books, Videos, or Apps to see what's available.

3. Tap a book, video, or app to open it.

4. If the item has not yet been downloaded, follow the orange progress bar as it downloads the book, video, or app to the Kindle Fire. If the item has a check mark, it's ready to be used.

5. The Back button takes you back to where you were.

6. The Search button lets you look for a book, app, or video on your account.

7. Tap and hold a book, video, or app to add it to your Favorites drawer.

8. Tap Add to Favorites.

9. Tap the star to see your Favorites drawer.

10. Tap an icon in your Favorites drawer to open it.

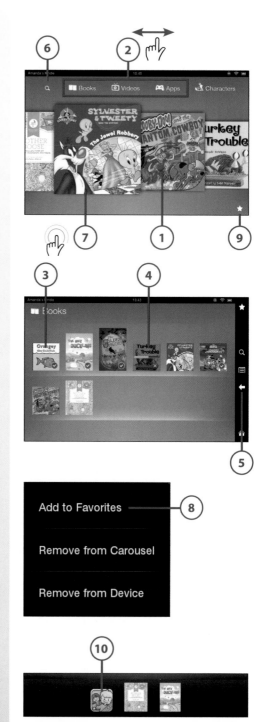

Removing Content

Although it seems illogical in such an otherwise controlled environment, your child can remove content from the Kindle Fire by tapping and holding an item and then choosing Remove from Device. If your child inadvertently does this, you must add the content to the profile again for your child to have access to it.

Navigation for Nonreaders

If your child is not yet reading, the Characters option on the Home screen lets your child choose books, videos, and apps based on the characters or theme of the content.

1. From the Home screen, tap Characters.

2. Choose a character or theme.

3. Choose a book or app to open.

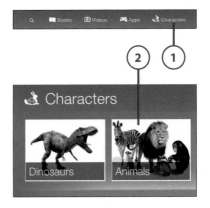

You Can't Choose How Content Is Categorized

The Characters groupings are not perfect. Content is sorted by Amazon, not by the parent, so you cannot control which characters and themes appear or whether a book, video, or app is included or excluded from that grouping. This feature should improve over time.

Exiting FreeTime

When it's your turn to use your
Kindle Fire, you can exit FreeTime.

1. Swipe down from the status bar
   to open Settings.

2. Tap Exit FreeTime.

3. Enter your parental controls password.

4. Tap OK.

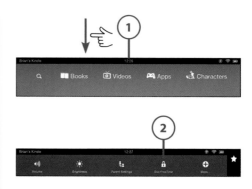

Changing Settings

Your child can access Settings to
change the volume on the Kindle
Fire and adjust the brightness of
the display. If your child attempts
to exit FreeTime or access any
other settings or parental controls, the Kindle Fire prompts your
child for a password.

Parental Controls for Older Children

If you have slightly older children, they might be ready to use the standard
Kindle Fire interface and have more freedom over how much time they spend
using the Kindle Fire. As a parent, however, you might still want to limit your
child's access to the Internet, e-mail, and other content.

The Kindle Fire's regular parental controls are much less restrictive than those
of Kindle FreeTime. In addition to blocking types of content or apps, you can
password-protect access to the Amazon Store and Instant Video, to prevent
your child from making unauthorized purchases or downloading inappropri-
ate content.

It's Not All Good

You Cannot Control Content by Rating

You can disable access to an entire content library, such as Videos or Books. However, you cannot control access to content by rating. If your child has access to the Videos library, for example, he or she can watch any video you have purchased on the Kindle Fire. If your child has access to the Books library, he or she can read that copy of *50 Shades of Gray* you purchased for your morning train commute. If you share your Kindle Fire with your children and worry about them accessing your content, consider limiting them to a FreeTime profile.

Setting a Parental Controls Password

Parental controls are password protected.

1. Swipe down from the status bar to open Settings.

2. Tap More.

3. Tap Parental Controls.

4. Tap On to turn on parental controls.

5. Create a parental controls password. If you've already created a password while setting up FreeTime for a younger child, use it here.

6. Type the password again to confirm it.

7. Tap Finish.

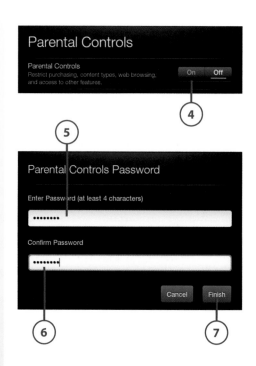

Managing Parental Controls Settings

After you enter your password, the Parental Controls screen displays several options to limit your child's use of the Kindle Fire.

1. Tap Web Browser to block or unblock access to Silk.

2. Tap E-mail, Contacts, Calendars to control access to those apps.

3. Tap the On or Off button for the Password Protect Purchases option. When this is On, purchases from the Amazon Store or the Amazon Shop app require a password. This includes in-app purchases.

4. Tap the On or Off button to password protect video playback. When On, this option requires a password to play Amazon Instant Video and Prime Instant Video.

5. Tap Block and Unblock Content Types to control access to content libraries.

6. Tap the Unblocked button to the right of any content type to toggle the button and block access to that content library.

7. Tap Back to return to the Parental Controls screen.

8. Tap Change Password to change the parental controls password.

9. Enter your current password.

10. Enter a new password.

11. Re-enter the new password to confirm it.

12. Tap Finish.

13. Tap the On or Off button to Password Protect Wi-Fi. When On, this setting requires the parental controls password to turn on Wi-Fi in order to download or stream content.

Turning Off Parental Controls

If you want to turn off parental controls, return to the Parental Controls screen and tap the Off button.

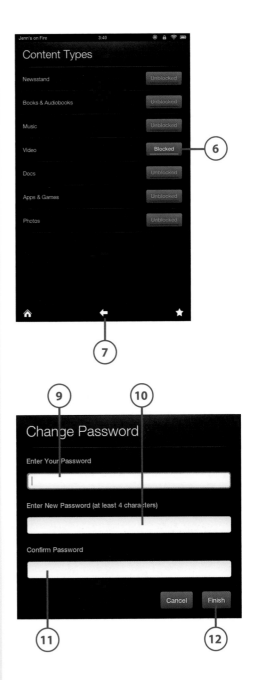

Index

A

accent marks, 36
accessing
 Add Account page, 250
 Amazon Cloud Drive, 49
 Cloud Drive files, 54-55
 Kindle Cloud Reader, 70-71
 Kindle Reader applications, 69
 Manage Your Kindle page, 80-81
 music controls, 163
accounts
 Amazon Prime accounts
  features, 44-45
  setting up, 45-47
 e-mail accounts, 249
  Add Account page, 250
  Microsoft Exchange accounts,
   adding, 256
  POP3 or IMAP accounts, adding,
   253-257
  removing, 260-261
  settings, 257-260
  webmail provider accounts,
   adding, 251-253
 Facebook, 226-227

 Skype, 235-237
 Twitter, 226-227
achievements (GameCircle), 243-244
Add Account page, 250
Adobe PDF reader, 272-273
ads in apps, 219
Album Only songs, 172
albums
 adding to playlists, 166
 browsing, 157
Amazon Cloud Drive. *See* Cloud Drive
Amazon Cloud Player. *See* Cloud Player
Amazon Instant Video, 66-68
Amazon Kindle Owners' Lending
 Library, 102
Amazon Kindle Store, 40-41, 100-101
Amazon Manage Your Kindle page. *See*
 Manage Your Kindle page
Amazon MP3 Settings, 65-66
Amazon Prime accounts
 features, 44-45
 setting up, 45-47
Amazon registration, 15
AOL accounts, adding, 251-253

approved e-mail addresses, 86
apps, 201. *See also* specific apps
  adding to Favorites, 209
  ads in, 219
  Apps library, browsing, 207-208
  Appstore, 201
    accessing from web browser, 202
    browsing apps, 202-203
    purchasing apps, 203-205
    test-driving apps, 205
    viewing apps, 203-205
    viewing subscriptions, 206-207
  browsing
    in Apps library, 207-208
    in Appstore, 202-203
  clearing application data, 214-215
  closing, 214
  force-stopping, 212-214
  free apps, 207
  installing, 208-209
  purchasing, 203-205
  test-driving, 205
  uninstalling, 210
  updating, 210-212
  viewing
    in Appstore, 203-205
    saved apps, 205
Apps library, browsing, 207-208
Appstore, 201
  accessing from web browser, 202
  browsing apps, 202-203
  purchasing apps, 203-205
  test-driving apps, 205
  viewing apps, 203-205
  viewing subscriptions, 206-207
archiving, disabling, 87
artists
  adding to playlists, 166
  browsing, 156-157
attachments (e-mail)
  opening, 268
  viewing, 267-268
Audible memberships, 125-126. *See also*
  audiobooks

audiobooks
  bookmarks, 127
  downloading, 125-126
  listening to, 126-127
  sleep timer, 128
Auto-Renewal, 207
AZW extension, 141

B

Before You Go page, 230-231
blocking content. *See* parental controls
Bluetooth accessories, 37-38
bookmarks
  audiobook bookmarks, 127
  ebook bookmarks
    adding, 119
    moving, 120
    removing, 119
  Silk bookmarks
    editing, 295-296
    following, 295
    to hyperlinks, 294
    viewing, 295
    to web pages, 293
books
  audiobooks
    bookmarks, 127
    downloading, 125-126
    listening to, 126-127
    sleep timer, 128
  Before You Go page, 230-231
  book information, editing
    downloading metadata, 143-145
    manually editing metadata, 146-147
  bookmarks
    adding, 119
    moving, 120
    removing, 119
  borrowing from Kindle Owners'
    Lending Library, 102
  browsing in library, 106
  buying, 100-101
  converting to MOBI format, 148-149
  covers, finding, 145
  definitions, looking up, 112-113

deleting, 84
downloading, 20-21, 106-107
   with Kindle Cloud Reader, 71-72
   with Manage Your Kindle page, 83-84
e-mailing to Kindle, 148, 151-153
font styles, changing, 111-112
formats
   converting to MOBI, 148-149
   EPUB, 148
   explained, 141
   non-MOBI formats, deleting, 149-150
highlights
   adding, 116
   availability, 113
   deleting, 118
   viewing, 117
immersion reading, 128-130
importing into Calibre, 140
lending, 103-104
metadata, downloading, 143-145
navigating, 109-111
notes
   adding, 114
   availability, 113
   deleting, 116
   editing, 115
   viewing, 115, 117
opening, 71-72, 108
page numbers, 109
pirated books, 142
reading, 73-74, 108-109
removing, 22, 107
sampling, 101
searching
   with Calibre, 141-142
   current item, 132-133
   X-Ray, 131-135
sideloading, 105, 148-151
text-to-speech capability, 130-131
transferring to Kindle Fire, 82-83, 150-151
viewing in Manage Your Kindle page, 81-82
Borrow for Free option, 102
borrowing books from Kindle Owners' Lending Library, 102
brightness (screen), adjusting, 30

browser. *See* Silk
browsing
   apps
      in Apps library, 207-208
      in Appstore, 202-203
   library, 106
   music
      by album, 157
      by artist, 156-157
      by song, 157
   videos in Video Store, 178-179
   web, 283
      bookmarks, 295-296
      history, 296
      hyperlinks, 289, 294
      Starter page, 284-285
      tabs, 291-293
      Trending Now suggestions, 285
      URLs, 285, 288-289
      web pages, 285-293
      web searches, 291
buttons
   power button, 10
   volume button, 10, 29
buying. *See* purchasing

C

cables, micro-USB-to-USB, 11
Calibre
   books
      converting to MOBI format, 148-149
      e-mailing, 151-153
      importing, 140
      non-MOBI formats, deleting, 149-150
      searching for, 141-142
      transferring to Kindle Fire, 150-151
   metadata
      downloading, 143-145
      editing manually, 146-147
   overview, 137-138
   plug-ins, 153
   updates, 137
   Welcome Wizard, 139
calibre-ebook.com, 138
calls, placing with Skype, 238-239

canceled subscriptions, reactivating, 89-90

canceling
music downloads, 160
subscriptions, 88-89

Carousel, 19-21

changing. *See also* editing
contacts name display, 280-281
contacts sort order, 280-281
font styles, 111-112
Kindle e-mail address, 85-87
payment information
Amazon purchases credit cards, 91-97
subscription credit cards, 93
screen timeout, 25-26
subscription delivery, 88

charging Kindle Fire, 11

chat, video chat, 234
calls, placing, 238-239
contacts, adding, 237-238
Skype setup, 235-237

checking device information, 30-31

child profiles, setting up, 305-306

children, setting up Kindle for
FreeTime, 303
accessing, 304-305
child profiles, 305-306
content management, 305-306
daily time limits, 308-309
exiting, 314
interface, 312-313
navigation for nonreaders, 313
parental controls passwords, 309-311
regular parental controls, 314
parental controls passwords, 315-316
settings, 316-317

choosing
e-mail folders, 262
inboxes, 261

clearing application data, 214-215

closing apps, 214

cloud, 20-22

Cloud Drive
accessing, 49
Amazon Cloud Drive application, downloading, 53-54

features, 47-48

files
accessing from Kindle Fire, 54-55
adding, 52-53
downloading to computer, 56
recovering, 52
saving to Kindle Fire, 55-56
folders
creating, 50
deleting, 51
recovering, 52
refreshing, 62
storing photos on, 232

Cloud Player
Amazon MP3 Settings, 65-66
features, 57
launching, 58
music
downloading to computer, 64
downloading to Kindle Fire, 63-65
importing, 58-60
streaming, 61-62
playlists, creating, 62

Cloud Reader, 70-71
accessing, 70-71
books
downloading, 71-72
opening, 71-72
reading, 73-74

Cloud view, 107

comments, sharing on social networks, 228

composing e-mail, 268-269

computers
downloading books to, 83-84
downloading Cloud Drive files to, 56
downloading Cloud Player music to, 64
transferring files from, 74
Linux, 76
Macs, 76
PCs, 75

configuring Kindle Fire. *See* setting up
Kindle Fire

connecting
to Bluetooth accessories, 37-38
to Facebook, 16
to Twitter, 16

to Wi-Fi networks
    listed Wi-Fi networks, 12-13
    unlisted Wi-Fi networks, 13-14
contacts
    adding to Favorites, 277
    adding to Skype, 237-238
    creating, 278-279
    editing, 280
    name display, 280-281
    sort order, 280-281
    viewing, 277
Contacts app, 277
    changing contacts sort order and name
      display, 280-281
    creating contacts, 278-279
    editing contacts, 280
    viewing contacts, 277
converting books to MOBI format, 148-149
copying
    hyperlinks, 289
    text, 35
    URLs, 288-289
copyright issues, 142
covers, finding, 145
credit card information, changing
    for Amazon purchases, 91-97
    for subscriptions, 93
cursor, positioning, 33
cutting text, 35

D

daily time limits, setting, 308-309
definitions, looking up, 112-113
deleting
    approved e-mail addresses, 86
    bookmarks, 119
    books, 84
    Cloud Drive folders, 51
    docs, 84
    downloaded files, 299
    downloaded videos, 196
    e-mail accounts, 260-261
    highlights, 118
    non-MOBI formats, 149-150

notes, 116
playlists, 169-170
sideloaded videos, 199
delivery preferences (music), 173
deregistering
    Kindle app, 96
    Kindle devices, 94
device information, checking, 30-31
device items, 20
Device screen, 30-31
diacriticals, entering, 36
digital rights management (DRM), 141
disabling doc archiving, 87
.doc documents
    editing, 276
    viewing, 274-275
docs. *See* documents
documents, 271
    archiving, disabling, 87
    deleting, 84
    PDF documents, viewing, 272-273
    sending to Kindle, 82-83
    spreadsheets
      editing, 276
      viewing, 275-276
    viewing, 81-82
    Word documents
      editing, 276
      viewing, 274-275
Documents to Go, 276
.docx documents
    editing, 276
    viewing, 274-275
double-tapping, 17
downloaded files
    removing, 22
    sharing, 298-299
downloading files, 20-21, 297-299
    Amazon Cloud Drive application, 53-54
    audiobooks, 125-126
    books, 106-107
      with Kindle Cloud Reader, 71-72
      with Manage Your Kindle page, 83-84
    Cloud Drive files
      to computer, 56
      to Kindle Fire, 55-56

metadata, 143-145

movies, 194

music

    canceling downloads, 160

    to computer, 64

    to Kindle Fire, 63-65

    monitoring downloads, 158-159

    playlists, 167-168

    TV shows, 195

DRM (digital rights management), 141

E

eBooks. *See* books

editing. *See also* changing

    book information

        downloading metadata, 143-145

        manually editing metadata, 146-147

    bookmarks, 295-296

    contacts, 280

    notes, 115

    playlists, 165

    spreadsheets, 276

    text, 34

    Word documents, 276

E Ink displays, 110

e-mail

    accounts, 249

        Add Account page, 250

        Microsoft Exchange accounts, 256

        POP3 or IMAP accounts, 253-257

        removing, 260-261

        settings, 257-260

        webmail provider accounts, 251-253

    addresses

        approved e-mail addresses, 86

        Kindle e-mail address, changing, 85-87

    attachments

        opening, 268

        viewing, 267-268

    composing, 268-269

    e-mail accounts, 249

        Add Account page, 250

        Microsoft Exchange accounts, adding, 256

        POP3 or IMAP accounts, adding, 253-257

        removing, 260-261

        settings, 257-260

        webmail provider accounts, adding, 251-253

    folders

        choosing, 262

        creating, 263

    inbox, choosing, 261

    loading, 264

    managing, 265

    reading, 266-267

    searching, 263

    selecting, 265

    sharing web pages with, 288

    synchronizing, 264

e-mailing books, 148, 151-153

eMusic.com, 174

enabling location, 301

entering

    accent marks, 36

    diacriticals, 36

    numbers, 35-36

    punctuation, 35-36

    text, 33

    URLs, 285

episodes of TV shows, buying, 184

EPUB, 141, 148

ES File Explorer, 219-220

ES Image Browser, 220

Evernote, 216-217

exiting Kindle FreeTime, 314

F

Facebook

    connecting to, 16

    Facebook app, 232-234

    photos, importing into Photos library, 231-232

    setting up, 226-227

    sharing to

        book highlights, 229-230

        comments, 228

reviews, 230-231
web pages, 287
Facebook app, 232-234
family, lending books to, 103-104
Favorites
adding, 23
apps, 209
contacts to, 277
rearranging, 24
removing, 24
fictionwise.com, 86
files
Cloud Drive files
accessing from Kindle Fire, 54-55
downloading to computer, 56
recovering, 52
saving to Kindle Fire, 55-56
uploading, 52-53
deleting, 299
downloading, 297-299
sharing, 298-299
transferring from computer, 74
Linux, 76
Macs, 76
PCs, 75
finding
books
with Calibre, 141-142
sideloaded books, 151
covers, 145
music, 160-161
Flash, 286
folders
Cloud Drive folders
creating, 50
deleting, 51
recovering, 52
e-mail folders
choosing, 262
creating, 263
following bookmarks, 295
font styles, changing, 111-112
force-stopping apps, 212-214

formats
EPUB, 148
MOBI format
converting to, 148-149
explained, 141
music formats, 174
non-MOBI formats, deleting, 149
free apps, 207
FreeTime, 303
accessing, 304-305
child profiles, 305-306
daily time limits, 308-309
exiting, 314
interface, 312-313
managing content on, 305-306
navigation for nonreaders, 313
parental controls passwords, changing, 309-311
preinstalled content, 311
friends
adding on GameCircle, 242-243
finding on GameCircle leaderboards, 245
lending books to, 103-104

G

GameCircle, 220, 239
achievements, 243-244
friends, adding, 242-243
game summaries, viewing, 246
identifying GameCircle games, 240-241
leaderboards, 244-245
profiles, creating, 241-242
games, 220
accessing, 221-222
GameCircle, 220, 239
friends, adding, 242-243
game summaries, viewing, 246
leaderboards, 244-245
profiles, creating, 241-242
identifying GameCircle games, 240-241
recommendations, 222
Games library, 221-222
General Settings (e-mail), 260
gestures, 17-18

Gmail accounts, adding, 251-253
Goodreads Sync plug-in, 153
Google searches, 134-135

H

hardware
    Bluetooth accessories, 37-38
    Kindle hardware, 10-11
HD (high-definition), 68, 181
headsets (Bluetooth), 37-38
hidden keyboard features, 36
high-definition (HD), 181
highlights
    adding, 116
    availability, 113
    deleting, 118
    sharing to social networks, 229-230
    viewing, 117
history (Silk), viewing, 296
Home screen
    Favorites
        adding items to, 23
        rearranging, 24
        removing items from, 24
    features, 19-20
    items
        adding to Favorites, 23
        downloading, 20-21
        removing, 22
        removing from Favorites, 24
    screen timeout, changing, 25-26
HootSuite, 234
Hotmail accounts, adding, 251-253
hyperlinks
    bookmarking, 294
    copying, 289

I

IMAP accounts, adding, 253-257
immersion reading, 128-130

importing
    books into Calibre, 140
    Facebook photos into Photos library,
        231-232
    music to Cloud Player, 58-60
inboxes, choosing, 261
initial setup
    Amazon registration, 15
    Facebook, connecting to, 16
    time zone, 14
    Twitter, connecting to, 16
    Wi-Fi networks, connecting to
        listed Wi-Fi networks, 12-13
        unlisted Wi-Fi networks, 13-14
installing apps, 208-209
Instant Video, 66-68
iTunes Store, 174

K

keyboard, 32
    accent marks, 36
    Bluetooth keyboards, 37-38
    cursor positioning, 33
    diacriticals, 36
    hidden features, 36
    punctuation and numbers, 35-36
    text
        copying/cutting and pasting, 35
        entering, 33
        selecting and editing, 34
kids, setting up Kindle for
    FreeTime, 303
        accessing, 304-305
        child profiles, 305-306
        content management, 305-306
        daily time limits, 308-309
        exiting, 314
        interface, 312-313
        navigation for nonreaders, 313
        parental controls password, 309-311
    regular parental controls, 314
        parental controls passwords, 315-316
        settings, 316-317
Kindle app, 82, 96

Kindle Cloud Reader, 70-71
  accessing, 70-71
  books
    downloading, 71-72
    opening, 71-72
    reading, 73-74
Kindle community, 226
  sharing book highlights to, 229-230
  sharing comments to, 228
  sharing reviews with, 230-231
Kindle devices
  deregistering, 94
  registering, 94
  renaming, 95
Kindle e-mail address, changing, 85-87
Kindle FreeTime, 303
  accessing, 304-305
  child profiles, 305-306
  daily time limits, 308-309
  exiting, 314
  interface, 312-313
  managing content on, 305-306
  navigation for nonreaders, 313
  parental controls passwords, changing,
    309-311
  preinstalled content, 311
Kindle Newsstand periodicals
  page view-enabled magazines, 121-123
  reading, 121-124
  subscribing to, 104-105
  text view, 123-124
  trial subscriptions, 105
Kindle Owners' Lending Library, 102
Kindle Paperwhite, 110
Kindle Personal Documents. *See* docs
Kindle Reader applications
  accessing, 69
  Kindle Cloud Reader
    accessing, 70-71
    opening and downloading books,
      71-72
    reading books, 73-74
Kindle Store
  books
    buying, 100-101
    sampling, 101
  searching, 40-41

L

landscape orientation, 28
Latest Additions playlist, 159
launching Cloud Player, 58
LCD screens, 110-111
leaderboards (GameCircle), 244-245
lending books, 103-104
links, copying, 288-289
Linux, transferring files from, 76
listed Wi-Fi networks, connecting to, 12-13
listening
  to audiobooks, 126-127
  to music, 162-163
loading e-mail, 264
location, enabling, 301
location numbers, 109
locking screen orientation, 28
looking up definitions, 112-113

M

Macs, transferring files from, 76, 151-153
magazines
  reading
    page view-enabled magazines,
      121-123
    text view, 123-124
  subscribing to, 104-105
Manage Your Kindle page, 79-80
  accessing, 80-81
  advantages of, 82
  books
    deleting, 84
    downloading to computer, 83-84
    sending to Kindle, 82-83
    viewing, 81-82
  docs
    deleting, 84
    disabling doc archiving, 87
    sending to Kindle, 82-83
    viewing, 81-82

e-mail addresses
    approved e-mail addresses, 86
    Kindle e-mail address, changing,
        85-87
Kindle app, deregistering, 96
Kindle devices
    deregistering, 94
    registering, 94
    renaming, 95
payment information, updating, 91-93
    Amazon purchases credit cards, 91-97
    subscriptions credit cards, 93
special offers, turning off, 97
subscriptions
    canceling, 88-89
    changing where subscription is deliv-
        ered, 88
    privacy settings, 91
    reactivating canceled subscriptions,
        89-90
    subscriptions credit cards, changing,
        93
Whispersync, turning off, 96-97
managing
    content on FreeTime, 305-306
    e-mail, 265
Media Transfer Protocol (MTP), 138
messages. See e-mail
metadata
    downloading with Calibre, 143-145
    manually editing, 146-147
micro-HDMI port, 11
Microsoft Exchange accounts, adding, 256
micro-USB cable, 84
micro-USB port, 10
micro-USB-to-USB cable, 11
MOBI format, 141
    converting books to, 148-149
    explained, 141
monitoring
    downloads, 297-298
    music downloads, 158-159
Movie Details screen (Video Store),
    179-180
movies. See videos
moving bookmarks, 120
MTP (Media Transfer Protocol), 138

music, 155
    browsing
        by album, 157
        by artist, 156-157
    buying, 171-172
    delivery preferences, 173
    downloading to Kindle Fire, 63-65
    downloads
        canceling, 160
        monitoring, 158-159
    formats, 174
    listening to, 162-163
    Music Store
        buying music, 171-172
        music delivery preferences, 173
        navigating, 170-171
        sampling music, 171-172
    Pandora, 217-219
    playback controls, 163
    playing, 161-163
    playlists
        adding artists/albums to, 166
        creating, 164-165
        deleting, 169-170
        downloading, 167-168
        editing, 165
        Latest Additions, 159
        playing, 167
        renaming, 169
    sampling, 171-172
    scrolling, 158
    searching, 160-161
    streaming from Cloud Player, 61-62
    uploading to Cloud Player, 58-60
Music Store
    buying music, 171-172
    music delivery preferences, 173
    navigating, 170-171
    sampling music, 171-172

N

name display of contacts, 280-281
navigating
    books, 109-111
    Music Store, 170-171

tabs, 292-293
web pages, 285-286
navigation for nonreaders, 313
Navigation menu, 19, 21
networks, Wi-Fi
    listed Wi-Fi networks, 12-13
    unlisted Wi-Fi networks, 13-14
The New Oxford American Dictionary, 112
newspapers
    reading, 123-124
    subscribing to, 104-105
Newsstand periodicals
    page view-enabled magazines, 121-123
    reading, 121-124
    subscribing to, 104-105
    text view, 123-124
    trial subscriptions, 105
nonreaders, navigation for, 313
notes
    adding, 114
    availability, 113
    deleting, 116
    editing, 115
    Evernote, 216-217
    viewing, 115, 117
notifications, viewing, 26-27
numbers
    entering, 35-36
    location numbers, 109
    page numbers, 109

O

OfficeSuite
    spreadsheets
        editing, 276
        viewing, 275-276
    Word documents
        editing, 276
        viewing, 274-275
OfficeSuite Pro, 276
opening
    books, 71-72, 108
    e-mail attachments, 268
    links in new tabs, 292

options, 27
Options bar, 27
organizing
    books, 105-106
    videos, 197
orientation, 28
overdrive.com, 102

P

page numbers, 109
Pandora, 217-219
parental controls
    FreeTime, 303
        accessing, 304-305
        child profiles, 305-306
        content management, 306-307
        daily time limits, 308-309
        parental controls password, changing,
            309-311
    regular parental controls, 314
        passwords, setting, 315-316
        settings, 316-317
Password Protect Purchases option, 316
Password Protect Video Playback option,
    316
Password Protect Wi-Fi option, 317
passwords, parental controls password,
    309-311
pasting
    text, 35
    URLs, 289
payment information, updating, 91-93
    Amazon purchases credit cards, 91-97
    subscriptions credit cards, 93
PCs, transferring files from, 75
PDF documents, viewing, 272-273
periodicals
    reading, 121-123
    subscribing to, 104-105
personal documents. See documents
photos
    Facebook photos, importing into
        Photos library, 231-232
    storing on Cloud Drive, 232

Photos library, importing Facebook photos into, 231-232

pinching, 18

pirated books, 142

playing

music, 61-62, 161-163

playlists, 167

playlists

adding artists/albums to, 166

creating, 62, 164-165

deleting, 169-170

downloading, 167-168

editing, 165

Latest Additions, 159

playing, 167

renaming, 169

plug-ins, Calibre plug-ins, 153

POP3 accounts, adding, 253-257

portrait orientation, 28

ports

micro-HDMI port, 11

micro-USB port, 10

positioning cursor, 33

power button, 10

powering on/off, 10

preinstalled content (FreeTime), 311

privacy settings, 91

profiles

child profiles, 305-306

GameCircle profiles, 241-242

protocols

IMAP, 257

POP3, 257

punctuation, entering, 35-36

purchasing

apps, 203-205

books, 100-101

movies, 67-68, 181-182

music, 171-172

subscriptions, 104-105

TV shows

complete seasons, 185

episodes, 184

from Prime Instant Video, 185-189

season TV Pass, 187-188

Q-R

Quick Links bar, 19

Quickoffice Pro, 276

radio, Pandora, 217-219

reactivating canceled subscriptions, 89-90

reading

books, 73-74, 108-109

e-mail, 266-267

immersion reading, 128-130

magazines

page view-enabled magazines, 121-123

text view, 123-124

newspapers, 123-124

PDF documents, 272-273

text-to-speech, 130-131

Word documents, 274-275

rearranging Favorites, 24

recovering

files on Cloud Drive, 52

folders on Cloud Drive, 52

refreshing Cloud Drive, 62

registering

Kindle devices, 94

with Amazon, 15

removing

bookmarks, 119

books, 107

downloaded items, 22

downloaded videos, 196

e-mail accounts, 260-261

Favorites items, 24

highlights, 118

notes, 116

videos from Watchlist, 193

renaming

Kindle devices, 95

playlists, 169

renting videos, 67-68, 181-182

reverse pinching, 18

reviews, sharing to social networks, 230-231

.rtf documents
    editing, 276
    viewing, 274-275

S

sampling
    books, 101
    music, 171-172
Saved for Later list, 205
saving
    Cloud Drive files to Kindle Fire, 55-56
    music
        to computer, 64
        to Kindle Fire, 63-65
screen brightness, adjusting, 30
screen orientation, 28
screen timeout, changing, 25-26
screens sharing, 38
scrolling, 18, 158
search engine, setting, 300
searching, 38
    Amazon Stores, 40-41
    books
        with Calibre, 141-142
        current item, 132-133
        X-Ray, 131-135
    e-mail, 263
    Google, 134-135
    library, 39
    music, 160-161
    Web, 39-40, 290-291
    Wikipedia, 134-135
seasons of TV shows, purchasing, 185
Seesmic, 234
selecting
    e-mail, 265
    text, 34
sending books/docs to Kindle, 82-83
setting up Kindle Fire
    Amazon Prime accounts, 45-47
    Amazon registration, 15
    child profiles, 305-306
    daily time limits, 308-309
    device information, 30-31

Facebook connections, 16
Kindle FreeTime, 303
    accessing FreeTime, 304-305
    child profiles, 305-306
    content management, 306-307
    daily time limits, 308-309
    parental controls password, 309-311
parental controls passwords, 315-316
screen brightness, 30
screen orientation, 28
search engine, 300
Skype, 235-237
social networks, 226-227
time zone, 14
Twitter connections, 16
volume, 29
Wi-Fi
    listed Wi-Fi networks, 12-13
    turning off, 32
    unlisted Wi-Fi networks, 13-14
settings
    contacts settings, 280-281
    e-mail accounts, 257-260
    fonts, 111-112
    parental control settings, 316-317
    screen brightness, 30
    screen orientation, 28
    Silk
        location, 301
        search engine, 300
    volume, 29
    Wi-Fi, 32
sharing
    book highlights to social networks,
        229-230
    comments to social networks, 228
    files, 298-299
    highlights to social networks, 229-230
    reviews to social networks, 230-231
    screen, 38
    web pages
        on Facebook, 287
        with e-mail, 288
sideloaded videos
    adding, 197
    deleting, 199
    watching, 198

sideloading, 80
  books, 105
    converting to MOBI format, 148-149
    deleting non-MOBI formats, 149-150
    e-mailing books, 151
    transferring books to Kindle, 150-151
  videos, 196-197
Silk, 283
  bookmarks
    editing, 295-296
    following, 295
    viewing, 295
  files
    deleting downloaded files, 299
    downloading, 297-299
    sharing, 298-299
  history, viewing, 296
  hyperlinks
    bookmarking, 294
    copying, 289
  settings
    location, 301
    search engine, 300
  Starter page, 284-285
  tabs, 291
    navigating, 292-293
    opening links in new tabs, 292
  Trending Now suggestions, 285
  URLs
    copying, 288-289
    entering, 285
    pasting, 289
  web pages
    bookmarking, 293
    copying links to, 288-289
    navigating, 285-286
    searching, 290
    sharing with e-mail, 288
  web searches, 291
Skype, 234
  calls, placing, 238-239
  contacts, adding, 237-238
  setting up, 235-237
sleep timer, 128

social networks, 225
  Facebook
    Facebook app, 232-234
    photos, importing into Photos library, 231-232
    setting up, 226-227
    sharing book highlights to, 229-230
    sharing comments to, 228
    sharing reviews with, 230-231
  Kindle community
    sharing book highlights to, 229-230
    sharing comments to, 228
    sharing reviews with, 230-231
  limitations, 226
  setting up, 226-227
  Twitter
    setting up, 226-227
    sharing book highlights to, 229-230
    sharing comments to, 228
    sharing reviews with, 230-231
    Tweetcaster, 234
songs. See music
sort order of contacts, 280-281
speakers
  Bluetooth speakers, 37-38
  built-in speakers, 11
special offers, turning off, 97
spreadsheets
  editing, 276
  viewing, 275-276
Starter page (Silk), 284-285
starting downloads, 297-298
status bar, 26
streaming
  music from Cloud Player, 61-62
  TV shows from Prime Instant Video, 185-189
  videos from Amazon Instant Video, 67-68
subscriptions
  adding to Favorites, 23
  Auto-Renewal, 207
  buying, 104-105
  canceling, 88-89
  changing where subscription is delivered, 88

privacy settings, 91
reactivating canceled subscriptions, 89-90
reading
    page view-enabled magazines, 121-123
    text view, 123-124
subscriptions credit cards, changing, 93
trial subscriptions, 105
viewing, 206-207
swiping, 18
synchronizing e-mail, 264

T

tabs
    navigating, 292-293
    opening links in new tabs, 292
tapping, 17
test-driving apps, 205
text
    copying/cutting and pasting, 35
    editing, 34
    entering, 33
    selecting, 34
    text-to-speech, 130-131
text-to-speech, 130-131
text view, 123-124
time zone, setting, 14
timeout setting, changing, 25-26
transferring
    books to Kindle Fire with Calibre, 150-151
    files from computer, 74
        Linux, 76
        Macs, 76
        PCs, 75
Trending Now suggestions (Silk), 285
trial subscriptions, 105
trophies (GameCircle), 243-244
turning off
    special offers, 97
    Whispersync, 96-97
    Wi-Fi, 32
TV Pass, 187-188

TV shows
    adding to Watchlist, 192-193
    downloading, 195
    purchasing
        complete seasons, 185
        episodes, 184
        from Prime Instant Video, 185-189
        season TV Pass, 187-188
    removing from Watchlist, 193
    sideloading, 196-197
    viewing details about, 182-183
    watching, 189-191
Tweetcaster, 234
Twitter
    connecting to, 16
    setting up, 226-227
    sharing book highlights to, 229-230
    sharing comments to, 228
    sharing reviews with, 230-231
    Tweetcaster, 234
.txt documents
    editing, 276
    viewing, 274-275

U

uninstalling apps, 210
unlisted Wi-Fi networks, connecting to, 13-14
updating, 12
    apps, 210-212
    Calibre, 137
    Kindle payment information, 91-93
    payment information
        Amazon purchases credit cards, 91-97
        subscriptions credit cards, 93
uploading
    Cloud Drive files, 52-53
    music to Cloud Player, 58-60
URLs
    copying, 288-289
    entering, 285
    pasting, 289
USB cable, 84
USB Mass Storage, 138

V

video chat, 234
  calls, placing, 238-239
  contacts, adding, 237-238
  Skype setup, 235-237
Video Store, 177
  movies
    browsing, 178-179
    renting/purchasing, 181-182
    standard versus high definition, 181
    viewing details about, 179-180
  TV shows
    buying by episode, 184
    buying complete seasons, 185
    season TV Pass, 187-188
    streaming from Prime Instant Video, 185-189
    viewing details about, 182-183
videos, 177. See also Video Store
  adding to FreeTime, 307
  adding to Watchlist, 192-193
  browsing in Video Store, 178-179
  deleting, 196
  getting from Amazon Instant Video, 67-68
  movies
    downloading, 194
    purchasing, 181-182
    renting, 181-182
    standard versus high definition, 181
    viewing details about, 179-180
    watching, 189-191
    X-Ray for Movies, 180
  organizing, 197
  password protection, 316
  removing from Watchlist, 193
  sideloaded videos
    adding, 197
    deleting, 199
    watching, 198
  TV shows
    buying by episode, 184
    buying complete seasons, 185
    downloading, 195
    season TV Pass, 187-188
    streaming from Prime Instant Video, 185-189
    viewing details about, 182-183
    watching, 189-191
  X-Ray for Movies, 180, 191-192
viewing
  apps in AppStore, 203-205
  bookmarks, 295
  books in Manage Your Kindle page, 81-82
  contacts, 277
  docs in Manage Your Kindle page, 81-82
  e-mail attachments, 267-268
  game summaries, 246
  highlights, 117
  history (Silk), 296
  notes, 115-117
  notifications, 26-27
  PDF documents, 272-273
  saved apps, 205
  spreadsheets, 275-276
  subscriptions, 206-207
  Word documents, 274-275
volume, adjusting, 29
volume button, 10, 29

W

watching
  movies, 189-191
  sideloaded videos, 198
  TV shows, 189-191
Watchlist, removing videos from, 193
web browser. See Silk
web browsing, 283
  bookmarks
    editing, 295-296
    following, 295
    viewing, 295
  history, viewing, 296

hyperlinks
bookmarking, 294
copying, 289
Starter page, 284-285
tabs, 291
navigating, 292-293
opening links in new tabs, 292
Trending Now suggestions, 285
URLs
copying, 288-289
entering, 285
pasting, 289
web pages
bookmarking, 293
copying links to, 288-289
navigating, 285-286
searching, 290
sharing on Facebook, 287
sharing with e-mail, 288
web searches, 39-40, 291
web pages
bookmarks
adding, 293
editing, 295-296
following, 295
viewing, 295
copying links to, 288-289
hyperlinks
bookmarking, 294
copying, 289
navigating, 285-286
searching, 290
sharing
on Facebook, 287
with e-mail, 288
URLs
copying, 288-289
entering, 285
pasting, 289
webmail provider accounts, adding, 251-253

Welcome Wizard (Calibre), 139
Whispersync, turning off, 96-97
Wi-Fi networks
listed Wi-Fi networks, 12-13
password protection, 317
turning off, 32
unlisted Wi-Fi networks, 13-14
Wikipedia, searching, 134-135
Word documents
editing, 276
viewing, 274-275

X-Y-Z

X-Ray, 131-135
X-Ray for Movies, 180, 191-192
.xls spreadsheets
editing, 276
viewing, 275
.xlst spreadsheets
editing, 276
viewing, 275

Yahoo! accounts, adding, 251-253

zooming in/out, 18

My Kindle Fire HD

Jim Cheshire and Jennifer Kettell

FREE Online Edition

Your purchase of *My Kindle Fire HD* includes access to a free online edition for 45 days through the **Safari Books Online** subscription service. Nearly every Que book is available online through **Safari Books Online**, along with thousands of books and videos from publishers such as Addison-Wesley Professional, Cisco Press, Exam Cram, IBM Press, O'Reilly Media, Prentice Hall, Sams, and VMware Press.

Safari Books Online is a digital library providing searchable, on-demand access to thousands of technology, digital media, and professional development books and videos from leading publishers. With one monthly or yearly subscription price, you get unlimited access to learning tools and information on topics including mobile app and software development, tips and tricks on using your favorite gadgets, networking, project management, graphic design, and much more.

Activate your FREE Online Edition at informit.com/safarifree

STEP 1:   Enter the coupon code: EACVHFH.

STEP 2:   New Safari users, complete the brief registration form. Safari subscribers, just log in.

If you have difficulty registering on Safari or accessing the online edition, please e-mail customer-service@safaribooksonline.com